ENDORSE[MENTS]

As evangelical Protestants we believe in [ ]
therefore, to discovering the meaning of the Scriptures, which means that we must study the Scriptures with intensity and rigor. This invaluable tool assists us in the task of careful exegesis and should be warmly welcomed.

—Thomas R. Schreiner, James Buchanan Harrison Professor
of New Testament Interpretation; Associate Dean,
The Southern Baptist Theological Seminary

Your life depends on the meaning of little words. "Soldier, get *in* your foxhole now!" If you think "in" means "out," you're dead! The stakes are even higher with "justified *by* faith." Or, "*in* this hope we were saved." Or, "created *in* Christ Jesus *for* good works." Or, "*On account of* these the wrath of God is coming." The *Interpretive Lexicon of New Testament Greek* by G. K. Beale and two others is dedicated to the conviction that crucial and glorious things in Scripture come into focus through rightly understanding the relationships signaled by these small words. This book wins my affection especially by correlating its definitions with the relational symbols I have been using for forty years. The book will accomplish a high purpose if it merely heightens the Bible-reader's expectancy that life-changing meaning is found not just in words and phrases, but in how words and phrases relate. Thank you, Dr. Beale and your team.

—John Piper, founder and teacher, desiringGod.org;
chancellor and professor of New Testament,
Bethlehem College and Seminary

One of the most challenging tasks in language acquisition is mastering the small words that are the warp and woof of an author's thought. Frequently, these words reveal the logical flow of a discourse and are thus crucial for understanding a given text. Gathering up the data from reference works, principally BDAG, Greg Beale and company have laid out the material in a way that focuses on the various kinds of logical relationships intended by the author. Systematically labeling each word in this lexicon according to sound discourse analysis principles, they have produced a volume whose time has come.

—Daniel B. Wallace, Professor of New Testament Studies,
Dallas Theological Seminary

Learning "discourse analysis" changed my life. For over thirty years I have been using variations of these charts and "handouts" to teach it to others as the most valuable tool we have. So I am very thankful for the labor of exegetical love that has gone into making this essential material available to future teachers and students.

—Scott Hafemann, Reader in New Testament, School of
Divinity, St. Mary's College, University of St. Andrews

This book with its analysis of prepositions, adverbs, particles, relative pronouns, and conjunctions is based on

A Greek-English Lexicon of the New Testament and Other Early Christian Literature, Second and Third Editions
by Walter Bauer, Frederick W. Danker, William F. Arndt, and F. Wilbur Gingrich

with references to
Greek Grammar Beyond the Basics: An Exegetical Syntax of the New Testament
by Daniel B. Wallace

as well as
Prepositions and Theology in the Greek New Testament: An Essential Reference Resource for Exegesis
by Murray J. Harris

an Interpretive Lexicon of

NEW TESTAMENT GREEK

ANALYSIS OF PREPOSITIONS, ADVERBS,
PARTICLES, RELATIVE PRONOUNS,
AND CONJUNCTIONS

G. K. Beale
Daniel J. Brendsel
William A. Ross

ZONDERVAN

An Interpretive Lexicon of New Testament Greek
Copyright © 2014 by Gregory K. Beale, William A. Ross, and Daniel Brendsel

This title is also available as a Zondervan ebook.
Visit www.zondervan.com/ebooks.

Requests for information should be addressed to:

Zondervan, 3900 Sparks Dr. SE, Grand Rapids, Michigan 49546

ISBN: 978-0-310-49411-9

Any Internet addresses (websites, blogs, etc.) and telephone numbers in this book are offered as a resource. They are not intended in any way to be or imply an endorsement by Zondervan, nor does Zondervan vouch for the content of these sites and numbers for the life of this book.

Cover design: John Hamilton Design
Interior design: Sherri L. Hoffman

Printed in the United States of America

HB 03.13.2024

INTRODUCTION

Meaningful extended communication is built on relationships (often logical) between the statements or propositions we make.[1] When someone says, "*Since* it is cold outside, *therefore* I am going inside," the first proposition ("it is cold outside") bears a certain logical relationship to the second proposition ("I am going inside"). In this instance we are helped in discerning the logical relationship by the key linking words "since" and "therefore." In other cases, the relationship between distinct propositions is not signaled by a linking word or other verbal sign. But the relationship still plausibly exists. So, for example, one might say, "It is cold outside; I'm going inside," and we may safely infer the same logical relationship as in our initial example, even though the words "since" and "therefore" are not present.

In communication we are always implicitly assuming or intuiting these relationships between clauses and sentences, whether we are aware of it or not. Everyday communication is thus built on meaningful relationships between the statements we make. Likewise, the New Testament's communication entails meaningful and logical relationships between statements or propositions. These relationships are especially apparent in genres using more explicit logical arguments — in particular, in the New Testament

---

1. In speaking of "statements" and "propositions," we are referring to any clause, consisting of a subject and a predicate. Importantly, clauses can be complete sentences or partial sentences, and independent or dependent. In this *Lexicon*, we deal partly with Greek prepositions. Prepositional phrases are not, strictly speaking, propositions (having a subject and predicate), but often a prepositional phrase will have the force of a proposition, especially when the object of the preposition is a verbal substantive (e.g., a verbal noun, a participle, or an infinitive). As a result, prepositions are important indicators of the logical flow of thought in a passage

epistles. They are a little more difficult, though not altogether impossible, to discern in, for example, poetic literature and narratives. Attempting to discern logical relationships between propositions (which some refer to as "discourse analysis") is a way of (1) making explicit what we might otherwise assume, in order (2) to test whether our assumptions are correct or incorrect or in need of refinements, with the result that (3) our understanding of a text is strengthened as we trace out an author's flow of thought in support of a main point.

With this in mind, this *Interpretive Lexicon of New Testament Greek* is intended as an aid for discerning logical relationships between propositions in order to enhance exegesis.[2] The specific help that this *Lexicon* provides is a taxonomy of functions performed by key Greek connecting words, particles, and other markers. In the example sentences given in the first paragraph above, the key words "since" and "therefore" helped to signal a certain kind of relationship (in the example, a logical relationship) between two clauses. Similarly in the Greek New Testament, words such as ἐπεί and οὖν signal certain meaningful relationships between clauses.

In short, this *Lexicon* examines and categorizes such key words found in the Greek New Testament that indicate relationships

---

2. For brevity's sake, this method, sometimes referred to as "discourse analysis," will not be discussed in detail here. See, further, e.g., John Beekman, John Callow, and Michael Kopesec, *The Semantic Structure of Written Communication* (5th ed.; Dallas: Summer Institute of Linguistics, 1981); Peter Cotterell and Max Turner, *Linguistics and Biblical Interpretation* (Downers Grove, IL: IVP Academic, 1989), 257–92; William D. Mounce, *A Graded Reader of Biblical Greek* (Grand Rapids: Zondervan, 1996), xii–xiii; Gordon Fee, *New Testament Exegesis* (Louisville: Westminster John Knox, 1993), 65–80; Steven E. Runge, *Discourse Grammar of the Greek New Testament: A Practical Introduction for Teaching and Exegesis* (Lexham Bible Reference Series; Peabody, MA: Hendrickson, 2010); Thomas R. Schreiner, *Interpreting the Pauline Epistles* (2nd ed.; Grand Rapids: Baker, 2011), 69–124. Also see the online materials provided by John Piper, especially the booklet "Biblical Exegesis: Discovering the Meaning of Scriptural Texts" (available at www.desiringgod.org/media/pdf/booklets/BTBX.pdf), and the website www.BibleArc.com for different approaches in line with our intent. The dominant influence of Tom Schreiner's and John Piper's approach is the unpublished work of Daniel P. Fuller.

between clauses and that are therefore integral to conveying and supporting a main idea (or main ideas) in communication. These words include prepositions, conjunctions, adverbs, particles, and relative pronouns, among others, as our title suggests. Note that while great effort has been made toward thoroughness in this *Lexicon*, we have not *exhaustively* treated all New Testament Greek prepositions, adverbs, particles, and the like. Rather, we have focused on the most common words, or words that are otherwise significant for discerning logical relationships between clauses.

For each Greek word considered, the various relationships between propositions that the word may represent or indicate are listed and various English renderings are suggested for translation. A very cursory explanation of analyzing logical relationships (i.e., a kind of discourse analysis) and the methodology used to label and categorize the use of Greek words is given below.

Logical Relationships between Clauses

The Greek words treated in this *Lexicon* represent or indicate various (logical) relationships between clauses. The table below lists and categorizes (see the far left columns with vertical text) the chief relationships that may exist between clauses. Additionally, the table offers brief working definitions of and abbreviations for these relationships, along with one example illustrating the core idea of the relationship. The abbreviations listed will be used throughout this *Lexicon* to denote the kinds of relationships between clauses/ propositions that a given Greek word may denote (see "Layout and Use of the Lexicon," below). The following definitions have been distilled from more nuanced discussions,[3] with the goal of making this *Lexicon* accessible to the nonexpert. Throughout the table we have linked our category labels/abbreviations to corresponding labels/abbreviations employed on BibleArc.com (appearing in parentheses after our labels in the table). However, we will be using our abbreviations throughout the lexicon itself.

---

3. See especially Beekman, Callow, and Kopesec, *Semantic Structure*. Page numbers in the following table correspond to such discussion of the relationships in chapter 8 of that book. The table itself has been influenced in many ways by Schreiner, *Pauline Epistles*, 100–113.

	Abbrev-iation	Definition
Coordinate Relationships	**Alt**	*Alternative* The relationship between propositions representing two or more differing possibilities or choices arising from a situation (83). E.g., "I can watch a movie *or* I can play golf."
	S	*Series* The relationship between propositions that independently contribute to a larger point (80–83).[4] E.g., "She ate breakfast *and* watched the news."
	P	*Progression* The relationship between propositions that lead toward (but do not cause) a goal or climax (83–85).[5] E.g., "He watered the plant *and* it grew *and* it bloomed."
Subordinate Relationships — **Support by Distinct Statement**	**∴**	*Inference* A proposition that is *logically* deduced from a preceding proposition (or set of propositions) that was *made as its basis*; the inverse of a Grounds relationship (on which see below) (106–7). E.g., "Jesus is God, *therefore* we worship him."
	C-E	*Cause-Effect* (aka *Action-Result* [= Ac-Res]) The relationship between propositions expressing an action and a consequent and resulting action or circumstance (similar to Inferences and Grounds, but dealing with *real world actions* rather than *ideas/reasoning*; similar to Means-End [on which see below], but *without* the intentionality of the agent in view) (102–3, 107). E.g., "The ball struck the window, *so that* it shattered."

---

4. Cf. Schreiner, *Pauline Epistles*, 100, for similar wording.
5. Cf. ibid., 101, for similar wording.

		Abbrev- iation	Definition
Subordinate Relationships	Support by Distinct Statement	C?-E	*Condition* (aka *Conditional* [= If-Th]) The relationship between propositions that explain a logical cause/means and its potential or hypothetical result/end, *with or without* intentionality from an agent (103 – 4). E.g., "*If* the ball strikes the window, *then* it will shatter."
		G	*Grounds* A proposition that gives the logical basis and support for *making* a preceding proposition; the inverse of an Inference relationship (on which see above) (106 – 7). E.g., "We worship Jesus *because* he is God."
		L	*Locative* A proposition that provides *orienting* information pertaining to the spatial or relational location, or source of another proposition (92). E.g., "She placed her coin *in the box*" (spatial); "They hold a grudge *against* their enemy" (relational).
		M-Ed	*Means-End* (aka *Action-Purpose* [= Ac-Pur]) The relationship between propositions expressing an action and its *intended* result/goal; often there is a focus on the agency or instrumentality involved in the initial action (similar to Cause-Effect, but with a view to *intentionality*; similar to Way-End, but concerning *agency/instrumentality*, not *manner*) (102 – 3). E.g., "I quit eating dessert *in order* to lose weight."
		T	*Temporal* A proposition that provides orienting information pertaining to the time of another proposition (93). E.g., "She received her allowance *after* she cleaned her room."

		Abbrev-iation	Definition
Subordinate Relationships	Support by Restatement	//	*Comparison* A proposition that expresses equivalence or close comparison (sometimes to show contrast) to another proposition (95, 97; Comparisons are at times functionally equivalent to a Way-End [100] or a Cause-Effect [100, 102–3]). On Cause-Effect see above, on Way-End see below. E.g., *"As* the Father sends me, *so likewise* I send you" (cf. John 20:21).
		-/+	*Negative-Positive* The relationship between propositions wherein one is denied so that another is affirmed; the affirmation (positive statement) is supported and emphasized *directly by* the denial (negative statement) (95–96). E.g., "It is not cold, *but rather* it is hot!"
		Ft-In	*Fact-Interpretation* (aka *Idea-Exploration* [= Id-Exp]) The relationship between two propositions (or sets of propositions) in which one provides orienting and/or clarifying information *exhausting* the semantic content of the other (93, 96). E.g., "A spiritual rock followed them, *and* the rock was Christ" (cf. 1 Cor 10:4).
		Gn-Sp	*General-Specific* (aka *Idea–Exploration* [= Id–Exp]) The relationship between two propositions (or sets of propositions) in which one narrows down to, and/or makes explicit, *parts* of the semantic content of the other (96–97). E.g., "Everyone in the class is intelligent, *and* Jennifer and Joe are certainly to be counted among them."

	Abbrev-iation	Definition
Subordinate Relationships — Support by Restatement	W-Ed	*Way-End* (aka *Action-Manner* [= Ac-Mn]) The relationship between one proposition stating an event/action and another proposition that describes the manner (1) in which an event occurred, (2) in which an agent carried out an action (similar to Means-End, but with a view to *manner*, not *agency/instrumentality*) (98 – 100). E.g., "I cleaned the house *in that* I vacuumed and dusted."
Subordinate Relationships — Support by Contrary Statement	Adv	*Adversative* (aka *Concessive* [= Csv]) A proposition that apparently negates or contradicts another proposition that nonetheless remains true (100 – 101, 104 – 5); the two propositions form a concessive relationship in which the contrary statement highlights the strength or surprising nature of the main statement; this may include a contrasting comparison notion (101), or combine with conditional notions (103 – 4), as noted in S-R and Q-A below. E.g., "*Even though* he is short, *nevertheless* he can dunk a basketball."
Subordinate Relationships — Support by Contrary Statement	S-R	*Situation-Response* The relationship between a proposition (or set of propositions) that elicits another proposition (or set of propositions), but not necessarily as a *cause*. This relationship is most common in narrative and dialogue with multiple agents, where responses and plot features are not strictly *caused* by the situation (85 – 91). N.B. This relationship occasionally includes a surprise element and thus may be subsumed under Adversative (on which see above). E.g., "Jesus performed many miracles *and* the multitudes believed."

		Abbrev-iation	Definition
Subordinate Relationships	**Support by Contrary Statement**	Q-A	*Question-Answer* The relationship between one (interrogative) proposition and another that is elicited by it in response either in argumentation or dialogue, but not as a cause (85 – 91). N.B. This relationship occasionally includes a surprise element and may be subsumed under Adversative (on which see above). E.g., "'Who do you say that I am?' ... 'You are the Christ'" (Mark 8:29).
Other		NLR	*No Logical Relationship* Used in the *Lexicon* to denote words (or word functions) that have no direct or perceivable bearing on the determination of logical relationships between propositions.

Layout and Use of the Lexicon

Several important points must be noted for the reader's successful use of this *Lexicon*. First, the interpretive categories and translational renderings offered in this *Lexicon* are grounded in and build on the work of the second and third editions of *A Greek-English Lexicon of the New Testament and Other Early Christian Literature* by Walter Bauer et al. Since the two editions have differing pagination and section labeling, the following format will be used to distinguish the two editions:

Page/section numbers appearing in normal font (e.g., "p. 90"; [B1]) are keyed to the 2000 edition (BDAG).

Page/section numbers appearing in *italicized font* (e.g., "*p. 75*"; [*II.1*]) are keyed to the 1979 edition (BAGD).

Wherever a given word entry contains references only in normal font (i.e., there is no italicized font in the entry), the reader should assume that both BDAG ('00) and BAGD ('79) list that information in the same section. In other words, italicized references to BAGD ('79) will *only* appear where pertinent information is given in a section *different* from BDAG ('00), so that the newer edition is our point of departure.

While this *Lexicon* is intended as a resource for exegesis, by its very nature it is a summary of the work of others. Accordingly, the authors urge the readers to refer consistently and carefully to BDAG ('00) and/or BAGD ('79) by making use of the page and section references we provide in each entry. This *Lexicon* can "stand alone" in one sense, but it is primarily intended to be used to facilitate the process of discerning logical relationships between propositions and thus exegetical analysis, which is done best with primary lexical and grammatical sources at hand. In reference to the latter, the entries in this *Lexicon* have also been keyed to relevant sections in two other books: (1) Daniel Wallace's *Greek Grammar beyond the Basics*, and (2) Murray Harris's *Prepositions and Theology in the Greek New Testament*.[6] Those who use this *Lexicon* are highly encouraged to cross-reference these valuable resources as well, where applicable.

On the next page is a sample entry (κατά), which is followed by an explanation of the features of entries in this *Lexicon* (the sample includes a footnote [n. 15] that is attached to the sample entry).

Immediately following the word designating the entry (in the case of the example below, κατά), page numbers are listed corresponding to BDAG ('00) in normal font and BAGD ('79) in italicized font. Again, if no italicized font is given, the reader may assume the reference is the same for both BDAG ('00) and BAGD ('79). For certain words, the symbol ▲ will appear before the page numbers, which designates that the word is listed as exhaustively

---

6. Daniel B. Wallace, *Greek Grammar beyond the Basics: An Exegetical Syntax of the New Testament* (Grand Rapids: Zondervan, 1996); Murray J. Harris, *Prepositions and Theology in the Greek New Testament: An Essential Reference Resource for Exegesis* (Grand Rapids: Zondervan, 2012).

κατά

pp. 511–13, *pp. 405–8*

PREPOSITION WITH GENITIVE

1. down from, on, into, throughout, down upon, toward, against; **L,**[15] **Gn-Sp,** or **Ft-In** [A] *[I]*

PREPOSITION WITH ACCUSATIVE

1. along, over, through, in, upon, toward, to, up to, by; **L** [B1] *[II.1]*
2. at, on, during, in, toward, about; **T** [B2] *[II.2]*
3. at a time, in detail, by; **Gn-Sp** or **Ft-In** [B3] *[II.3]*
4. for the purpose of, for, to; **M-Ed** [B4] *[II.4]*
5. according to, in accordance with, in conformity with, in (such and such) a manner; **W-Ed, Gn-Sp,** or **Ft-In** [B5a, bβ, 6] *[II.5a, bβ, 6]*
6. in accordance with, on the basis of, on account of, because of; **G** or **C-E** [B5aδ] *[II.5aδ]*
7. in accordance with, just as, similarly; // or **G** [B5aδ, bα] *[II.5aδ, bα]*
8. (functioning, with its object, like an adjective, possessive pronoun, or genitive noun; see, e.g., Rom 11:21: "the natural branches"); **NLR** [B7] *[II.7]*

Wallace — spatial diagram, p. 358; basic uses and significant passages, pp. 376–77; independent clauses introduced by a prepositional phrase, p. 658.

Harris [pp. 147–60] — basic meaning, p. 147; phrases involving κατά, pp. 147–52; κατά denoting correspondence or conformity, pp. 152–54; κατά denoting opposition, pp. 154–55; distributive κατά, pp. 155–57; some ambiguous examples, pp. 157–60; κατά in compounds, p. 160.

---

15. This Locative function of κατά with the genitive demonstrates how the "logically orienting information" provided may be either spatial or relational: e.g., "Throw a rock *against* the wall" (spatial, [A1] *[I.1]*), and "Hold a grudge *against* an enemy" (relational [A2] *[I.2]*). In this sense, this relationship may be more broadly (i.e., less specifically) labeled **Gn-Sp** or **Ft-In**. See further "Logical Relationships between Clauses" in the Introduction above.

examined in BAGD ('79), either in terms of its usage in Greek literature or in the Greek New Testament.[7]

Throughout the *Lexicon*, if applicable, the word's different syntactical functions will be denoted using capitalized font (e.g., κατά has two syntactical functions: PREPOSITION WITH GENITIVE and PREPOSITION WITH ACCUSATIVE). Some words may have only one label since they have only one function (e.g., ὅταν below in the *Lexicon*, which is labeled only TEMPORAL PARTICLE). In the sample above, the two syntactical function labels separate the listed translational renderings/logical relationships into two categories.

If there is a division into syntactical function(s), within each syntactical function, we group translational ranges of meaning by boldface numbers (**1.**, **2.**, **3.**, etc.) that present further information by category. The numbers and the information presented in each category are organized roughly according to the word's discussion in BDAG ('00). Note that these boldface numbers are not identical to BDAG/BAGD's boldface numbers, since we may divide up one or more of BDAG/BAGD's ranges of meaning into two or more ranges of meaning. Similarly, while the vast majority of translational renderings come from BDAG/BAGD, occasionally we have formulated our own.

Most prominently, translational renderings are suggested for the word according to suggested logical relationships and a given syntactical function (e.g., in the case of κατά above, "down from, on, into ...," in category one [**1.**] under PREPOSITION WITH GENITIVE). These various renderings are followed by a semicolon (;), after which appear abbreviations denoting the logical relationship(s) possibly signaled by the Greek word. In the sample

---

7. Only BAGD ('79) marks entries as exhaustively represented from Greek literature or from the New Testament. BDAG ('00) states that "the proliferation of papyri and new editions of early Christian literature suggests caution about certainty respecting completeness of citation. The use of asterisks (indicating completeness of citation, either of the NT or the Apostolic Fathers or both) at the end of entries has therefore been abandoned [in the 2000 edition]. But students can count on completeness of citation of all except the most common words appearing in the main text of the 27th edition of Nestle" (p. x; also see p. xxix in BAGD ['79]).

entry of κατά above, only one numbered category (**1.**) appears under PREPOSITION WITH GENITIVE, listing several translational renderings, after which it is proposed that κατά + genitive may denote the various logical relationships of a Locative (**L**), General-Specific (**Gn-Sp**), or Fact-Interpretation (**Ft-In**). In category two (**2.**) under PREPOSITION WITH ACCUSATIVE, however, only one relationship is given (**T** [= Temporal]). In many instances it is difficult to narrow the possible relationships with great specificity. Often when engaged in interpretation of a specific text the reader will be left to decide between several possible relationships, a decision among which will depend on exegetical context.

This again is why it is so important that one refer to BDAG ('00) and/or BAGD ('79), using the page numbers and sections provided. After possible relationships for a word are presented (e.g., **L, Gn-Sp,** or **Ft-In**) in a numbered category, the BDAG ('00) and BAGD ('79) sections that correspond to the logical relationships we have listed are given in brackets (e.g., [B1] *[II.1]*). Often BDAG ('00) and BAGD ('79) employ different sectionalizing schemes. In the sample entry of κατά above, for instance, section B in BDAG ('00) corresponds to section II in BAGD ('79), while both editions denote subsections with Arabic numerals (1, 2, 3, etc.). In all instances, our entries will list the corresponding sections in both editions that pertain to the relationship(s) in view.

Several other items must be noted regarding our entries. First, we do not discuss *every section* of every word entry in BDAG/BAGD treated here, but have left sections unaddressed when we have judged that they are not pertinent to this *Lexicon* (i.e., if certain functions of a word play no clear part in signaling a logical relationship between propositions). In some cases, for clarity's sake, we have listed the abbreviation **NLR** in a numbered line, to state expressly that certain words (or word functions) signal, at least by themselves, "no logical relationship" between propositions (e.g., numbered category eight [**8.**] in the sample entry above).[8]

---

8. When a word (or word function) in the *Lexicon* is labeled with the "No Logical Relationship" symbol (NLR), this does not suggest that any proposition in which the word appears has no logical relationship to its surrounding

Second, the reader may occasionally note that a specific BDAG/BAGD subsection is listed in two or more different numbered categories in the same entry of this *Lexicon*, thus linking the subsection with two or more logical relationships (see, e.g., numbered categories six [**6.**] and seven [**7.**] in the sample entry of κατά above). This occurs where we have discerned differing possible logical relationships in a single subsection but have no way of identifying the logical relationships with any greater specificity. In these cases, the reader will be further helped by consulting BDAG/BAGD.

Third, the sections from BDAG/BAGD are listed *inclusively* in our entries. This means that, unless otherwise noted, the sections we list for a given numbered category and relationship(s) include any and all subsections in BDAG/BAGD (e.g., merely listing A includes all subsections [A1, A2, A3, etc.], as well as all subsubsections [A1α, A1β, A1γ, etc.]). Note that occasionally we have seen the need for footnotes in word entries to provide clarifying information. For example, in the entry above, footnote fifteen ([15]) appears in numbered category one (**1.**) under PREPOSITION WITH GENITIVE. Also, sometimes translational renderings given will include one or more words in parentheses, which designates where an additional nuance in meaning occasionally occurs, according to the stylistic conventions of BDAG/BAGD.

Finally, in the space below word entries we have provided information relevant to the word as found in Wallace or Harris, if either work discusses it, along with page references.

Broader Methodological Matters

It may be helpful, before concluding, to touch on two important features of language to keep in mind when using this book.

First, clause relationships are merely *signaled* by words, since words themselves are not what create or contain semantic relationships. The *content*, or meaning, that an author wishes to

---

propositions, but only that the specific word under consideration does not function to signal (at least on its own) what relationships may be at work. In such instances, logical relationships between propositions must be determined based on other factors (e.g., other verbal markers, context).

communicate in a text has a direct influence on the *words* he or she chooses to use. Thus, the "shape" of the *words* in the text — their order, the author's selection of one word over other possible words, and the decision of what to make explicit or to leave implicit — represents and is determined by *the author's meaning in context*, not vice versa. For our purposes, the words we treat in this *Lexicon* indicate logical relationships between propositions; however, as alluded to earlier, those same relationships may exist even where the connecting words we discuss are not textually present.

A word is, in this sense, like a road sign that says "Now leaving Cheltenham: Welcome to Philadelphia." The sign itself is not the city or the *reason* one is leaving Cheltenham and entering Philadelphia. But it *represents* the reality of being in a new location as well as the reality of Philadelphia, both of which would remain whether or not the road sign was there to mark them. More to the point, it would not make sense to say that one must be leaving Cheltenham and entering Philadelphia (and that Philadelphia exists) *only because* the road sign is there to say so. Again, the sign states something that remains true whether or not the sign itself exists to be seen. In the same way, there will be instances where relationships exist between propositions in the text *without* the presence of one of the words in this *Lexicon* to alert the exegete to that relationship.[9] The practical consequence is that this *Lexicon* is by no means an exhaustive guide to meaningful relationships between propositions, which occur with or without connecting words to signal them. It is only an attempt to categorize the relationships ordinarily *represented* by a given word *when such a word appears in the text.*

A second feature of language to bear in mind is that word meaning and clause relationships are tied to their context. For on the one hand, it is true that the reality of traveling from Cheltenham to Philadelphia remains a reality whether or not the sign "Now leaving Cheltenham: Welcome to Philadelphia" exists. But

---

9. For a fuller discussion, see Beekman, Callow, and Kopesec, *Semantic Structure*, esp. p. 78.

on the other hand, that reality is *not true* unless one is in the proper context, namely, the right geographical location. That specific road sign and the reality it represents is patently *untrue* if it were in, say, Chicago.

Two implications may be drawn from this. First, although the words in this *Lexicon* are "signs" with real meaning potential, they (and all words) do and must have reference to their context to make sense or have such meaning. Thus, there is a finite (but large) number of contexts in which a specific word may be used validly. Our Philadelphia road sign could sit at the intersection of *any* Cheltenham street with the city border, but it could not sit at a crossroads in Chicago. In short, a specific word cannot mean *anything*, but has limited meaning potential, and context will help determine specifically how that meaning potential is brought to realization in a text. A word must mean something definite in each specific context, and the possibility of that word's meaning is limited in scope by its ordinary, conventional use in a given language and community. Otherwise, communication would be impossible.

A second implication of word meaning and clause relationships being tied to context is that since words have a range of meanings, they *can* validly represent different meanings in different contexts. For instance, the word "play" in English means something quite different in the sentences "The play begins at seven" and "Please play safely." In both propositions, the word is used validly, effectively communicating meaning to the listener, but the context determines the specific meaning of the "same" word within its semantic range. That is because, again, the "same" word can mean different things depending on context.

Matters become slightly more complex, however, when dealing with words that function to indicate the *relationships* between clauses. Flip to any entry of this *Lexicon* and note that almost all the Greek words have multiple groups of possible translational renderings, and that these groups are often tied to multiple relationships (which are often logical). Just as words have a range of translational renderings that is narrowed by context, they simultaneously have a range of possible logical functions in discourse as well, and any particular logical function in a given text must be determined by context. When considering words like the ones in this *Lexicon*, we have moved more from the realm of "mere" lexical *translation* into *interpretation* of the relationships between clauses, although these tasks are never totally separate.[10] To decide which English semantic relational word should represent the Greek, the exegete must pay attention not only to the possible range of translational renderings of the Greek *words*, but to the possible range of the *relationships* at the discourse level that are signaled by those words. The difference between the "meaning" of a given word and the meaning of clausal relationships is subtle but important.

In short, this is an *Interpretive Lexicon* because it is *for* interpretation and *is* an interpretation. Just as the English translations of the Greek words given in this *Lexicon* are approximate and potential interpretive paraphrases, so are the relationships suggested, since the Greek entries are clearly *not* situated in context. Instead, the entries attempt to organize the relationships ordinarily represented by the words based on their occurrences in various contexts according to BDAG/BAGD. This is yet another reason why the reader will do well to refer consistently and carefully to BDAG/BAGD in order to understand a word's use in context.

It is also worth noting that the authors of BDAG/BAGD have not everywhere employed the exact same terminology for the relationships as we do. As a result, this *Lexicon* must be, at base, an attempt to organize, even an interpretation of, the information provided in BDAG/BAGD (i.e., not merely a summary). This distillation of the data in BDAG/BAGD is particularly needed in the occasional entry where BDAG/BAGD is not organized strictly by similar types of relationships as employed in this *Lexicon*,

---

10. In translating, for example, any particular ὅτι, we have to determine not only how it is best translated *lexically* in English — "that" or "because" or something else — but also how it signals a *relationship* between what precedes it and what follows it. These two decisions are distinct but inseparable parts of the translation process.

where differing terminology occurs, or where no distinct position is taken by BDAG/BAGD pertaining to relationships. This is especially true for the Cause-Effect, Grounds, and Inference relationships, which can be difficult to distinguish and categorize without context.[11] Wherever these situations arise, and given all that has been said thus far in this introduction, it is up to the *exegete* to do the interpretive legwork, despite the helps provided in this *Lexicon*. Therefore, we again recommend that BDAG/BAGD be consulted directly, using the page numbers listed where there is room for interpretive question.

By this time the reader may be wondering what the point of this *Lexicon* is in the face of such complexity. Fortunately, despite the many difficulties of language and translation, it *is* possible to demonstrate with clarity (1) the meaning of a great majority of conventional uses of words, and (2) how those words express logical relationships that language uses to communicate. That is the goal to which this *Lexicon* is a means, in hopes of aiding more accurate and streamlined linguistic and exegetical work.

We must acknowledge our indebtedness in this project to the work of Tom Bazacas and Scott Minnich. It was their initial project in the late 1980s as an independent study with G. K. Beale at Gordon-Conwell Theological Seminary that formed the basis of the present work. Their "Interpretative Lexicon" was formatted in much the same way as the present work, but was of course keyed only to BAGD ('79). This *Lexicon* is a thorough review, revision, and expansion of their excellent work.

In a similar spirit as Bauer et al., we cite here a quote by the famous lexicographer Samuel Johnson from the preface to his dictionary: "Every other author may aspire to praise; the lexicographer can only hope to escape reproach, and even this negative recompense has been yet granted to very few."[12] Although we do not claim to have undertaken the lexicographical task de novo in this

---

11. So, e.g., ἐκ τούτου may introduce either a Grounds or an Inference, though BDAG/BAGD does not distinguish at all between these potential relationships. See entry below for further discussion.

12. Cited in BDAG ('00), vii.

book, and although we have striven for consistency and correctness, compiling the information herein has been a time-consuming and complicated task. Doubtless we have made errors along the way, either objectively (page number, sections, formatting, etc.) or subjectively (logical relationship labeling or translational rendering). We therefore invite the attentive reader to submit suggested changes via email to Interpretive.Lexicon@gmail.com.

ABBREVIATIONS*

Logical Relationships in Alphabetical Order

Adversative	Adv (Csv)	Inference	∴
Alternative	Alt (A)	Means-End	M-Ed (Ac-Pur)
Cause-Effect	C-E (Ac-Res)	Negative-Positive	-/+
Comparison	// (Cf)	No Logical Relationship	NLR
Condition	C?-E (If-Exp)	Progression	P
General-Specific	Gn-Sp (Id-Exp)	Question-Answer	Q-A
		Series	S
Fact-Interpretation	Ft-In (Id-Exp)	Situation-Response	S-R (Sit-R)
		Temporal	T
Grounds	G	Way-End	W-Ed (Ac-Mn)
Locative	L		

Symbols in Alphabetical Order

∴	Inference	L	Locative
//	Comparison	M-Ed	Means-End (Action-Purpose)
-/+	Negative-Positive		
Adv	Adversative (Concessive)	NLR	No Logical Relationship
Alt	Alternative	P	Progression
C?-E	Condition (Conditional)	Q-A	Question-Answer
C-E	Cause-Effect (Action-Result)	S	Series
		S-R	Situation-Response
Ft-In	Fact-Interpretation (Idea-Explanation)	T	Temporal
		W-Ed	Way-End (Action-Manner)
G	Grounds		
Gn-Sp	General-Specific (Idea-Explanation)		

---

*The abbreviations/labels appearing in parentheses and italics are the ones used on BibleArc.com. We reference them here to better facilitate the use of this lexicon with the resources available there. We will be using our abbreviations throughout the lexicon itself.

an Interpretive Lexicon of

NEW TESTAMENT
GREEK

ἀλλά

pp. 44 – 45, *pp. 38 – 39*

Adversative Particle (or conjunction)

1. on the contrary, yet, but, rather (often after a negative or μέν); -/+ [1, 3, 4b]
2. but, yet, nevertheless, rather; **Adv** or **Alt** [2, 3, 4a] *[2, 3, 4, 5]*
3. now, then (usually in dialogue: Acts 10:20); **S-R** [5] *[6]*
4. so, therefore, accordingly (rare: Eph 5:24?); ∴ [5] *[6]*
5. certainly, at least; **NLR** [4a] *[4]*

Wallace — independent clauses with a coordinating conjunction, p. 657; common coordinating conjunctions, p. 669; logical contrastive (adversative) and correlative (paired) conjunctions, pp. 671 – 72; logical emphatic conjunctions, p. 673.

ἅμα

▲ p. 49, *p. 42*

Adverb

1. at the same time (often with a temporal participle); **T** or **S** [1] *[1a]*
2. together with (sometimes with σύν); **NLR** [2a] *[1b]*

Used as a Preposition

1. together with (rare: Matt 13:29); **T** [2b] *[2]*

Harris — "improper" prepositions in Hellenistic Greek with chart, p. 241; ἅμα, p. 242.

ἄν

pp. 56 – 57, *pp. 48 – 49*

Particle

1. (if) … then (in an apodosis or second part of a conditional sentence), (if) … would (esp. in adversative conditional scenarios; cf. Luke 7:39); **C?-E** [I.a, I.b] *[1, 2]* (cf. εἰ, p. 277 [1, 2], *p. 219 [I]*)

2. when, whenever, as soon/often as, every time (usually with subj. and combined with other temporal particles or conjunctions, e.g., ὅτε, ἡνίκα, ὡς; see entries below); **T** [I.c] *[3]*

3. (following ὅπως; see entry below); **M-Ed** [I.d] *[4]*

4. (sometimes in place of ἐάν [rare: John 13:20; Acts 9:2], on which see ἐάν below); **NLR**

Wallace — dependent (subordinate) clauses with conditional subjunctive and the construction of the conjunction ἐάν, pp. 469 – 70; the potential optative mood, pp. 483 – 84; dependent, indefinite relative clauses, p. 660; the structure of conditions, p. 689; second class (contrary to fact) conditions, pp. 694 – 96; fourth class (less probable future) conditions, pp. 699 – 701.

ἀνά

pp. 57 – 58, *p.* 49

PREPOSITION WITH ACCUSATIVE

1. among, between, in the middle, in the midst of; **L** [1]

2. in turn, in sequence; **NLR** [2]

3. each, apiece; **NLR** [3]

Wallace — basic distributive use with genitive, p. 364.

Harris [pp. 45 – 48] — NT uses of ἀνά, pp. 45 – 46; ἀνὰ μέσον and ὁ θρόνος in Revelation, pp. 46 – 48; ἀνά in compounds, p. 48.

ἄνευ

p. 78, *p.* 65

PREPOSITION WITH GENITIVE

1. without; **NLR** [a, b] *[1, 2]*

Harris — chart of "improper" prepositions in Hellenistic Greek, p. 241; ἄνευ, pp. 242 – 43; notable uses of selected "improper" prepositions: ἄνευ, pp. 253 – 55.

ἀνθ' ὧν

▲ see ἀντί, p. 88, *pp. 73 – 74*

Preposition with relative pronoun used as a conjunction
1. because; **G** [4] *[3]*
2. therefore, wherefore, so then (rare: Luke 12:3);
   ∴ [5] *[3]*

Wallace — adverbial/conjunctive use of the relative pronoun with a preposition, p. 342.

Harris — basic idea and NT use, p. 49.

ἀντί

pp. 87 – 88, *pp. 73 – 74*

Preposition with genitive
1. as, for, in place of, in exchange for, instead of, in behalf of; **Gn-Sp** or **NLR** [1, 2, 3]
2. instead (see Jas 4:15); -/+ or **Alt** [3]

See also entries for ἀνθ' ὧν *above and* ἀντὶ τούτου *below.*

Wallace — basic uses and significant passages, pp. 365 – 68; comparison with ὑπέρ, the issue of atonement, and other significant passages, pp. 383 – 89.

Harris [pp. 49 – 56] — basic idea and NT use, p. 49; use as equivalent, pp. 49 – 50, exchange, p. 50; substitution, pp. 50 – 51; important NT uses, pp. 51 – 56; ἀντί in compounds, p. 56.

ἀντὶ τούτου

▲ see ἀντί, p. 88, *p. 73*

Preposition with demonstrative pronoun used as a conjunction
1. because of, for this reason, therefore (rare: Eph 5:31);
   ∴ [4] *[3]*

Harris — basic idea and NT use, p. 49.

ἄντικρυς

▲ p. 89, *p. 74*

ADVERB USED AS PREPOSITION WITH GENITIVE
1. opposite (rare: Acts 20:15); L

Harris — "improper" prepositions in Hellenistic Greek
with chart, pp. 240 – 41; ἄντικρυς, p. 243.

ἀντιπέρα

▲ p. 90, *p. 75*

ADVERB USED AS PREPOSITION WITH GENITIVE
1. opposite (rare: Luke 8:26); L

Harris — chart of "improper" prepositions in Hellenistic
Greek, p. 241; ἀντιπέρα, p. 243.

ἀπέναντι

▲ p. 101, *p. 84*

ADVERB USED AS PREPOSITION WITH GENITIVE
1. opposite, before, in the presence of; L [1b] *[1]*
2. against, contrary to; W-Ed or Gn-Sp *[2]*

Harris — chart of "improper" prepositions in Hellenistic
Greek, pp. 240 – 41; ἀπέναντι, p. 243.

ἀπό

pp. 105 – 7, *pp. 86 – 88*

PREPOSITION WITH GENITIVE
1. from, away from, out from; L [1b, 2a, 3, 4] *[I.2, II.1,
III, IV]*
2. because of, as a result of, for, with; C-E or G [5] *[V]*
3. from ... (on/until), since, when, beginning with
(sometimes with ἕως, μέχρι, ἄχρι, or the rel. pron.);
T [2b] *[II.2]*
4. of, from; Gn-Sp [1f] *[I.6]*
5. with, with the help of (rare: Rev 18:15); W-Ed [5b] *[V.2]*

Wallace — ablatival genitive of separation pp. 107 – 9, and
of source (origin) p. 109; ἀπό and the genitive of time,
p. 123; ἀπό with pronouns, p. 343 (see also entry for ἀφ᾽ οὗ
below); spatial diagram, p. 358; basic uses and significant
passages, p. 368.

Harris [pp. 57 – 67] — relation of ἀπό to ἐκ, pp. 57 – 58;
ἀπὸ θεοῦ, pp. 58 – 60; ellipses with (pregnant) ἀπό,
pp. 60 – 61; ἀπό in Paul's epistolary salutations, p. 62; other
notable instances, pp. 62 – 67; ἀπό in compounds, p. 67.

ἄρα

▲ p. 127, *pp. 103 – 4*

PARTICLE

1. then, so, consequently, as a result, you see, therefore;
∴ or C-E [1, 2b] *[1, 2, 4]*
2. then (introducing the apodosis, or second part of a
conditional sentence [as a complement to εἰ; see entry
below]); C⸴-E [2a] *[3]*
3. (after ἐπεί) then, otherwise; NLR [1a] *[3]*
4. (combined with οὖν; see also entry below) therefore,
then, so then; P or ∴ [2b] *[4]*

Wallace — independent clauses introduced by a coordinating conjunction, p. 658; and by logical inferential
conjunctions, p. 673.

ἆρα

▲ p. 127, *p. 104*

INTERROGATIVE PARTICLE

1. then (rare: Luke 18:8; Acts 8:30; Gal 2:17); T,[1] C⸴-E,
and/or Q-A

---

1. In such cases, ἆρα introduces a main clause, while pointing back to a
Temporal clause (T).

ἄτερ

▲ p. 148, *p. 120*

PREPOSITION WITH GENITIVE

1. without, apart from; L or **W-Ed**

Harris — chart of "improper" prepositions in Hellenistic Greek, p. 241; ἄτερ, p. 243.

ἀφ᾿ ἧς/οὗ

see ἀπό, p. 105, *p. 87*; ὅς, p. 727, *p. 585*

PREPOSITION WITH GENITIVE RELATIVE PRONOUN

1. when once, since, until (the time when) (rare: Luke 13:25; Col 1:6, 9); **T** (ἀπό [2bγ] *[II.2c]*; ὅς [1kζ] *[I.11f]*)

Wallace — adverbial/conjunctive use of the relative pronoun with a preposition, p. 343.

Harris — relation of ἀπό to ἐκ, pp. 57 – 58; ἀπὸ θεοῦ, pp. 58 – 60; ellipses with (pregnant) ἀπό, pp. 60 – 61; ἀπό in Paul's epistolary salutations, p. 62; other notable instances, pp. 62 – 67; ἀπό in compounds, p. 67.

ἄχρι(ς)

▲ pp. 160 – 61, *pp. 128 – 29*; see also ὅς, p. 727, *p. 585*

PREPOSITION WITH GENITIVE USED AS A CONJUNCTION

1. until (also with rel. pro. οὗ); **T** [1] *[1a, 2]* (see also ὅς [1kζ] *[I.11f]*)
2. as far as; L [2] *[1b, 2]*

Wallace — genitive after certain prepositions, p. 136; subjunctive in indefinite temporal clause, p. 479; use with future and aorist tense, p. 568 n. 4; adverbial temporal conjunctions, p. 677.

Harris — chart of "improper" prepositions in Hellenistic Greek, p. 241; ἄχρι(ς), pp. 243 – 44.

γάρ

pp. 189 – 90, *pp. 151 – 52*

CONJUNCTION

1. for, because; **G** [1]
2. for, you see, moreover, now; **Ft-In** or **Gn-Sp** [2] *[2, 4]*
3. therefore, so, then, certainly, by all means; ∴ [3] *[3, 4]*
4. indeed, to be sure, certainly (similar to δέ); **S** or **P** [2] *[4]*
5. but, although (rare: Rom 5:7); **Adv** or **Alt** [2] *[4]*

Wallace — independent clauses introduced by a coordinating, explanatory conjunction, p. 658; introducing subordinate causal clauses, p. 662 n. 12; common Greek coordinating conjunctions, pp. 668 – 69; logical explanatory, inferential, and causal conjunctions, pp. 673 – 74.

γέ

p. 190, *pp. 152 – 53*

ENCLITIC PARTICLE

1. yet, at least; **Adv** [aα] *[1]*
2. even, indeed; **Ft-In** or **NLR** [aβ] *[2]*
3. though, although (with καί or καίτοι); **Adv** [bγ, δ] *[3c, d]*

See also entry for μενοῦνγε *below.*

Wallace — emphatic conjunctions, p. 673.

δέ

p. 213, *p. 171*

PARTICLE USED AS A CONJUNCTION

1. and, as for, then, so, at the same time, and also (with καί), *untranslated*; **S** or **P** [1, 2, 3, 5] *[1c, 2, 3, 4]*
2. but (sometimes with καί: but also/even), rather, on the other hand; **Adv**, -/+, or **Alt** [4a, b, c, 5] *[1a, b, d, 4]*
3. now, that is; **Ft-In** or **Gn-Sp** [2]
4. and, then, now, so; **C-E** or **S-R** [2, 4a] *[not in BAGD]*

5. then (introducing an apodosis, or second part of a conditional sentence) (rare: 2 Pet 1:5, see v. 3 for protasis); C?-E [4d] [1e]

In combination with μέν, see entry for μέν below.

Wallace — the article in place of or amplifying the personal pronoun, pp. 211 – 13; independent clauses introduced by a coordinating, connective conjunction, p. 657, and correlative conjunction, p. 658; common Greek coordinating conjunctions, p. 669; logical conjunctions: ascensive conjunctions, p. 670, connective (continuative, coordinate) conjunctions, p. 671, contrastive (adversative) conjunctions p. 671; correlative (paired) conjunctions, p. 672, explanatory conjunctions, p. 673.

δεύτερος, δεύτερα, δεύτερον
pp. 220 – 21, *p. 177*

ORDINAL NUMBER SOMETIMES USED AS AN ADVERB
1. second (esp. in a sequence or list); P or NLR [1, 2] [3, 4]

δή

▲ p. 222, *p. 178*

PARTICLE
1. now, then, therefore; ∴, Ft-In, or NLR [1, 2]

Wallace — emphatic conjunctions, p. 673.

διά

pp. 223 – 26, *pp. 179 – 81*

PREPOSITION WITH GENITIVE
1. through, via, throughout; L [A1] [A.I]
2. throughout, through, during, after; T [A2] [A.II]
3. by, via, through (the agency of); M-Ed [A3a, d, e, f, A4] [A.III.1a, d, e, f, A.III.2]
4. by, in; W-Ed [A3b, c] [A.III.1b, c]
5. via, by; C-E or G [A3d, e, 5] [A.III.1d, e, A.IV]

PREPOSITION WITH ACCUSATIVE

1. because of, for the sake of, for this reason (with, e.g., τοῦτο; also see entry for διότι below); C-E, ∴,[2] or G [B2] [B.II]
2. through (rare: Luke 17:11); L [B1] [B.I]
3. why? (in interrogative clauses, often with τί); Q-A [B2b] [B.II.2]

See also διὰ τό + inf., and διὰ τοῦτο, below

Wallace — genitive of agency, p. 126; dative of agency and the intermediate agent, p. 164; demonstrative pronouns used as conceptual antecedent/postcedent, p. 333; spatial diagram, p. 358; basic uses and significant passages, pp. 368 – 69; passive voice, prepositions, and agency, pp. 431 – 34; adverbial, causal use of the infinitive, pp. 596 – 97; articular infinitives with a governing preposition, p. 610; independent clauses introduced by a prepositional phrase, p. 658.

Harris [pp. 69 – 82] — origin and basic idea, p. 69; notable instances of main uses: temporal, pp. 69 – 70, means/instrument/agent, pp. 70 – 72, cause or ground, pp. 72 – 76, attendant/accompanying/prevailing circumstances and manner, pp. 77 – 80, purpose?, pp. 80 – 82; διά in compounds, p. 82.

διὰ τό + inf.

see διά p. 226, p. 181

PREPOSITION WITH ACCUSATIVE ARTICULAR INFINITIVE
1. because; G [B2c] [B.II.3]

Wallace — infinitive, adverbial uses, cause, pp. 596 – 97; articular infinitives, p. 610.

---

2. See entry for διά τοῦτο below for further discussion.

διὰ τοῦτο

See διά pp. 225 – 26, *p. 181*; cf. διότι p. 251, *p. 199*

PREPOSITIONAL PHRASE USED AS A CONJUNCTION

1. because of this, for the sake of this, for this reason;
   C-E, ∴, G, or Gn-Sp[3] [B2] [B.II] (see also entry for
   διότι below)

Wallace — demonstrative pronouns used as conceptual
antecedent/postcedent, p. 333; independent clauses introduced by a prepositional phrase, p. 658.

διό

p. 250, *p. 198*

CONJUNCTION

1. therefore, for this reason; ∴

Wallace — classification of independent clauses: introduced
by a coordinating conjunction, pp. 657 – 58; inferential
conjunctions, p. 673.

διόπερ

▲ p. 250, *p. 199*

CONJUNCTION

1. therefore, for this very reason; ∴

διότι

▲ p. 251, *p. 199*

CONJUNCTION

1. because, for; C-E or G [1, 3]

---

3. Note that διά τοῦτο can refer to an antecedent idea/statement, and so
be used to introduce an Inference. On the other hand, when τοῦτο refers to a
postcedent idea/statement, the proposition in which διά τοῦτο appears will be
followed by a Grounds. Such instances of διά τοῦτο followed by a Grounds may
also be viewed as General-Specific relationships, since the phrase in which διὰ
τοῦτο appears may also be described as a general statement, followed by a specific statement identifying the grounds (that is, identifying the referent of τοῦτο).

2. therefore (= διὰ τοῦτο, on which see διὰ τοῦτο above; rare: Acts 13:35); ∴ [2]

3. that; (rare: Rom 8:21 [*variant*]); **Ft-In** or **Gn-Sp** [4]

Wallace — logical inferential conjunctions, p. 673; adverbial causal conjunctions, p. 674.

ἐάν

pp. 267 – 68, *p. 211*

CONJUNCTION

1. if (introducing the protasis, or first part of a conditional statement); **C?-E** [1a, b, c] *[I.1, 2, 3]*

2. whenever, when; **T** [2] *[I.1d]*

3. (sometimes in place of ἄν [rare: Matt 5:19; 1 Cor 16:6], on which see ἄν above); **NLR** [3] *[II]*

Wallace — subjunctive used in dependent (subordinate) clauses and the construction of the conjunction ἐάν, pp. 469 – 71; dependent, indefinite relative clauses, p. 660; third class conditional clauses, p. 663; common Greek subordinating conjunctions with subjunctive, p. 669; adverbial conditional conjunctions, p. 675; conditional sentences, pp. 680 – 87; structural categories of conditional sentences, p. 689; the third class condition, pp. 696 – 99; the controversy between systems of classification of conditional sentences, pp. 705 – 12.

ἐάνπερ

▲ see ἐάν p. 268, *p. 211*

CONJUNCTION

1. if indeed, if only, supposing that (rare: Heb 3:6; 6:3); **C?-E** [1cγ] *[I.3c]*

Wallace — see sections in entry for ἐάν above.

ἐγγύς

▲ p. 271, *p. 214*

ADVERB
1. near, close to; **L** [1, 3]
2. near, soon; **T** [2]

Harris — chart of "improper" prepositions in Hellenistic Greek, p. 241; ἐγγύς, p. 244.

εἰ

pp. 277 – 79, *pp. 219 – 20*

PARTICLE (OFTEN COMBINED WITH OTHER WORDS)
1. if, unless; **C?-E** [1, 3, 6a, b, c, d, f, g, h, iα, j, k, l, m, n, 7] *[I, III, VI.1, 2, 3, 5, 6, 7, 8a, 9, 10,11, 12, VII]*
2. that; **Ft-In** or **Gn-Sp** [2, 5b] *[II, V.2]*
3. since, if (formally a conditional clause); **G** [3] *[III]*[4]
4. if ... (or) if, whether ... or; **Alt** [6o] *[VI.13]*
5. even if, even though, although (εἰ καί), only (see εἰ μή in Gal 1:7; possibly 1 Cor 7:17); **Adv** [6e, iβ] *[VI.4, 8b]*
6. but (see Matt 12:4; 1 Cor 7:17); -/+ [6iβ] *[VI.8b]*
7. (marker of assertion without apodosis); **NLR** [4] *[IV]*

See also entry for μέν *below.*

Wallace — conditional indicative, pp. 450 – 51; the construction of the conjunction ἐάν, pp. 469 – 70; the conditional optative, p. 484; conditional, adverbial, dependent clauses, p. 663; common Greek subordinating conjunctions, p. 669; logical explanatory conjunctions, p. 673; adverbial conditional conjunctions, p. 675; overview of conditional sentences, pp. 680 – 87; structural categories of conditional sentences, p. 689; first, second, third, and fourth class con-

---

4. In such εἰ clauses, the ground or basis is *assumed to be true for the sake of argument* but is not necessarily true in reality. Note that Wallace argues that εἰ in "first class conditions" (εἰ + indicative in the protasis) should *never* be translated "since." See Wallace, pp. 690 – 94.

ditions, pp. 690 – 701; the controversy between the systems of conditional classification, pp. 705 – 12.

εἵνεκεν

"Improper" preposition; see ἕνεκα, ἕνεκεν, εἵνεκεν *below.*

εἴπερ

see εἰ p. 279, *p. 220*

PARTICLE

1. if indeed, if after all, granted (rare: Rom 3:30); C?-E [6l] [VI.11]

Wallace — first class conditions using εἴπερ, p. 694.

εἰς

pp. 288 – 91, *pp. 228 – 30*

PREPOSITION WITH ACCUSATIVE

1. into, in, toward, to, among, near, on, at; L [1, 10c] [1, 6e, 9a]
2. to, until, on, for, throughout; T [2]
3. into, to, in order to, toward, at, by (sometimes combined with, e.g., ὅ, τί, [αὐτὸ] τοῦτο); M-Ed or C-E [4a, d, e, f, 6, 10a] [4a, d, e, f, 6a, b, 9b]
4. for, to, with respect to, with reference to; **Gn-Sp** or **Ft-In** [5]

See also εἰς (αὐτὸ) τοῦτο; εἰς τό + inf.

Wallace — substitution for predicate nominative, p. 47; the dative of destination, pp. 147 – 48; spatial diagram, p. 358; basic uses and significant passages, pp. 369 – 71; adverbial use of the infinitive with εἰς (purpose and result clauses), pp. 590 – 94; εἰς τό + infinitive, p. 611; independent clauses introduced by prepositional phrases, p. 658.

Harris [pp. 83 – 102] — origin and NT use, p. 83; its relation to πρός, pp. 83 – 84; its relation to ἐν, pp. 84 – 88; telic εἰς, pp. 88 – 90; consecutive/ecbatic εἰς, p. 90;

causal εἰς?, pp. 90 – 92; significant phrases using εἰς,
pp. 92 – 100; significant successive instances of εἰς,
pp. 100 – 101; ambiguity of meaning, pp. 101 – 2; εἰς in
compounds, p. 102.

εἰς (αὐτὸ) τοῦτο

see εἰς p. 290, *p. 229*

PREPOSITIONAL PHRASE

1. for this (very) reason, for this (very) purpose (rare:
   Col 4:8; 2 Cor 5:5); **M-Ed** or **Gn-Sp**[5] [4f]

Harris — see esp. pp. 99 – 100; origin and NT use,
p. 83; its relation to πρός, pp. 83 – 84; its relation to ἐν,
pp. 84 – 88; telic εἰς, pp. 88 – 90; consecutive/ecbatic εἰς,
p. 90; causal εἰς?, pp. 90 – 92; significant phrases using
εἰς, pp. 92 – 100; significant successive instances of εἰς,
pp. 100 – 101; ambiguity of meaning, pp. 101 – 2; εἰς in
compounds, p. 102.

εἰς τό + inf.

see εἰς p. 290, *p. 229*

PREPOSITION WITH ACCUSATIVE ARTICULAR INFINITIVE

1. so that; **C-E** [4e]
2. in order to/that; **M-Ed** [4f]

Wallace — infinitive, adverbial uses, purpose, pp. 590 – 91;
result, pp. 592 – 93; articular infinitives, p. 611.

---

5. Εἰς τοῦτο generally indicates that some purpose or goal is in view (hence
Means-End), but since the demonstrative pronoun refers to an antecedent or
postcedent idea/statement, the prepositional phrase may also be understood to
be a part of a General-Specific relationship. Usually in such General-Specific
relationships, a general statement identifies an action and a purpose (by way of
εἰς τοῦτο), which is then followed by a statement (introduced with ἵνα) specify-
ing the purpose. See, e.g., Rom 14:9: "To this end (εἰς τοῦτο) Christ died and
lived again [General], *that* (ἵνα) he might be Lord both of the dead and of the
living [Specific]."

εἶτα

▲ p. 295, *pp. 233 – 34*

ADVERB
1. then, next; **P** or **C-E** [1]
2. furthermore, then, next; **P** [2]

εἴτε ... εἴτε

see εἰ p. 279, *p. 220*

PARTICLE COMBINED WITH ANOTHER PARTICLE
1. if ... (or) if, whether ... or; **Alt**[6] [60] *[VI.13]*

Wallace — see references in entry for εἰ above, especially p. 669.

ἐκ

pp. 295 – 98, *pp. 234 – 36*

PREPOSITION WITH GENITIVE
1. from, out of, away from; **L** [1, 2, 3a, b, c, 3g, 4aα, β, γ, δ] *[1, 2, 3a, b, c, d, 3g, 4aα, β, γ, δ]*
2. from, of, because of; **G** or **C-E** [3a, d, e, i] *[3a, e, f, i]*
3. with, by means of (rare: Luke 16:9); **M-Ed** [3a, f]
4. from, from ... on, for; **T** [5]
5. (various other uses); **NLR** [6]

See also ἐκ τούτου.

Wallace — the genitive ablative and the five-case system, p. 77; partitive ("wholative") genitive, pp. 84 – 86; genitive of material, pp. 91 – 92; ablatival genitive, pp. 107 – 9; genitive of source (origin), pp. 109 – 10; genitive of means, p. 125; spatial diagram, p. 358; basic uses and significant passages, pp. 371 – 72; table of NT agency expression, p. 432; passive, impersonal means, pp. 434 – 35; independent clauses introduced by prepositional phrases, p. 658.

---

6. In many cases, the Alternative relationship denoted here exists between two "if" clauses, which *together* form a protasis to some apodosis.

Harris [pp. 103 – 13] — introduction, p. 103; basic
signification, p. 103; range of figurative uses, pp. 103 – 5;
important constructions using ἐκ, pp. 105 – 10; other significant instances of ἐκ, pp. 110 – 13; ἐκ in compounds, p. 113.

ἐκ τούτου

▲ see ἐκ p. 297, *p. 235*

PREPOSITION WITH GENITIVE USED AS A CONJUNCTION
1. for this reason, therefore, as a result; (rare: John 6:66)
   C-E or ∴[7] [3e] *[3f]*

Wallace — independent clauses introduced by prepositional phrases, p. 658.

ἐκεῖ

p. 301, *p. 239*

ADVERB
1. there; **L** (when complementing ὅπου or οὗ)[8] or **NLR** [1]

ἐκτός

▲ p. 311, *p. 246*

PREPOSITION WITH GENITIVE
1. outside; **L** or **NLR** [2] *[2a]*
2. except; **C?-E**[9] or **NLR** [3b] *[2b]*

ADVERB
1. except (with εἰ μή); **C?-E** [3a] *[1]*

Harris — chart of "improper" prepositions in Hellenistic Greek, p. 241; ἐκτός, p. 244; notable uses of selected
"improper" prepositions: ἐκτός, pp. 255 – 59.

---

7. These logical relationships only apply in those instances in which τούτου
in ἐκ τούτου is used as a demonstrative pronoun (e.g., 1 John 4:6), not as an
adjective (e.g., Matt 26:29).

8. In such cases, ἐκεῖ introduces a main clause, while pointing back to a
Locative clause (L) introduced by ὅπου or οὗ.

9. Exceptions function as negative conditions: "If not [i.e., except] for this or
that instance, X would always be true." See also 1. below, under Adverb.

ἔμπροσθεν

▲ p. 325, *p. 257*

ADVERB

1. in front (of), toward the front, forward, farther, ahead;
   L [1a, 2] *[1]*

USED AS A PREPOSITION WITH GENITIVE

1. in front of, before, in the presence of, in the sight of;
   L [1b] *[2]*

Wallace — genitive after certain prepositions, p. 136.
Harris — possible Semitic influence on NT prepositional
use, p. 36; chart of "improper" prepositions in Hellenistic
Greek, p. 241; ἔμπροσθεν, p. 244; notable uses of selected
"improper" prepositions: ἔμπροσθεν, pp. 259–60.

ἐν[10]

pp. 326–30, *pp. 258–61*

PREPOSITION WITH DATIVE

1. in, among, on, at, near, before, in the presence of,
   within, into; L [1, 3, 4] *[I.1, 3, 4a, b, 5, 6]*
2. in, with; **W-Ed, Gn-Sp,** or **Ft-In**[11] [2, 4, 7, 8, 11]
   [I.2, 4b, d, 5, III.1, 2, IV.1a, 6e]
3. with, by (including ἐν ᾧ, on which see entry below);
   M-Ed or **W-Ed** [5, 6] *[I.4c, III.1, 2, IV.6c]*
4. because, for, on account of; **G** or **C-E** [8, 9] *[I.2, III.3,
   IV.6d]*

---

10. The entry for ἐν is significantly revised in BDAG ('00). Much is rearranged, new material is introduced, and some portions are removed. Making things more complex, fractions of entries in BAGD ('79) have been resituated into different entries in BDAG ('00). As a result, and given the wide use of ἐν in the NT, our entry, while covering the majority of the word's functions, is somewhat limited. Consult Bauer in both editions for unclear cases.

11. Depending on the context, certain phrases using ἐν might be categorized legitimately as an L, W-Ed, or Gn-Sp relationship, which has made categorizing this entry difficult. See, for example, "in the Spirit" (Rom 8:9) or "in him [Christ]" (Phil 3:9). See further "Logical Relationships between Clauses" in the Introduction, and the discussions in Harris.

5. in, while, when, on, at, (mean)while, during; **T** [7, 10]
   [*II, IV.6b*]
6. (various other uses); **NLR** [8, 12] [*I.2, IV.2, 3, 4a, b*][12]

See also entries for ἐν τῷ + inf. and ἐν ᾧ below.

Wallace — ἐν and the genitive of association, pp. 128 – 29;
dative of destination, pp. 147 – 48; dative of time,
pp. 155 – 57; dative of manner, pp. 161 – 62; dative of
content, pp. 170 – 71; spatial diagram, p. 358; basic uses
and significant passages, pp. 372 – 75; table of NT agency
expression, p. 432; impersonal means, pp. 434 – 35;
infinitive of result with prepositions, p. 593; infinitive
of time (contemporaneous), p. 595; infinitive of means,
pp. 597 – 98; articular infinitives, p. 611; adverbial, dependent clauses of manner/means, p. 664.

Harris [pp. 115 – 36] — extended NT use and ultimate
disappearance, pp. 115 – 16; versatility, pp. 116 – 17;
encroachment on other prepositions, pp. 117 – 18;
main uses: locatival, temporal, instrumental, agency,
causal, attendant circumstance/accompaniment, respect,
ἐν = εἰς, exegetical ambiguities, pp. 118 – 22; key phrases,
pp. 122 – 36; ἐν in compounds, p. 136.

ἐν τῷ + inf.

see ἐν pp. 329 – 30, *pp. 260 – 61*

PREPOSITION WITH DATIVE ARTICULAR INFINITIVE

1. so that, with the result that (rare: Heb 3:12);
   C-E (see Wallace, pp. 592 – 93)
2. while, as, when; **T** [7, 10c] [*II.3*]
3. in that, by, whereby; **W-Ed** [7] [*III.1b*]

Wallace — infinitive, adverbial uses, result, p. 593;
contemporaneous time, p. 595; means, pp. 597 – 98;
articular infinitives, p. 611.

---

12. In some cases of ambiguity or overlap, the same sections have also been
listed under a specific relationship (e.g., section 8. [*I.2, IV.4a*]). Refer to each if
in doubt about a particular use of ἐν.

ἐν ᾧ

see ἐν pp. 329 – 30, *p. 261*

PREPOSITION WITH DATIVE RELATIVE PRONOUN USED AS
A CONJUNCTION
1. wherein, in what/which; **Gn-Sp** or **Ft-In** [7] *[IV.6a, e]*
2. while, as long as; **T** [10c] *[IV.6b]*
3. whereby; **W-Ed** [5b] *[IV.6c]*
4. because, since; **G, C-E,** or ∴ [9a] *[IV.6d]*
5. whereas; **Adv,** *[IV.6e]*

Wallace — relative pronouns with embedded demonstratives, p. 340; adverbial/conjunctive use of relative pronouns, pp. 342 – 43.

ἔναντι

▲ p. 330, *p. 261*

ADVERB USED AS A PREPOSITION WITH GENITIVE
1. before, opposite, in the eyes of; **L** [1, 2]

Harris — chart of "improper" prepositions in Hellenistic Greek, p. 241; ἔναντι, p. 244.

ἐναντίον

▲ p. 330, *pp. 261 – 62*

ADJECTIVE USED AS A PREPOSITION WITH GENITIVE
1. before, in the sight of, in the presence of; **L** [1]

Adverbial with article, see entry for τοὐναντίον *below.*

Harris — chart of "improper" prepositions in Hellenistic Greek, p. 241; ἐναντίον, p. 244.

ἕνεκα, ἕνεκεν, εἵνεκεν

▲ p. 334, *p. 264*

PREPOSITION WITH GENITIVE
1. because of, on account of, for the sake of; **G** [1]
2. for this reason (ἕνεκα τούτου/τούτων); ∴ [2]
3. in order that; (rare: 2 Cor 7:12) **M-Ed** [2]

Wallace — genitive after certain prepositions, p. 136.

Harris — chart of "improper" prepositions in Hellenistic Greek, p. 241; ἕνεκα, p. 245.

ἐντεῦθεν

▲ p. 339, *p. 268*

ADVERB

1. from here; **L** or **NLR** [1]
2. from this (rare: Jas 4:1); **Ft-In, Gn-Sp,** or **C-E** [2]

ἐντός

▲ pp. 340 – 41, *p. 269*

ADVERB USED AS A PREPOSITION WITH GENITIVE

1. inside, within, within the limits of; **L**

Harris — chart of "improper" prepositions in Hellenistic Greek, p. 241; ἐντός, p. 245; notable uses of selected "improper" prepositions: ἐντός, pp. 260 – 61.

ἐνώπιον

▲ p. 342, *pp. 270 – 71*

PREPOSITION WITH GENITIVE

1. before, in the sight of, in the presence of, among; **L** [1, 2] *[1, 2, 5a]*
2. against (rare: Luke 15:18); **L** [4a] *[5b]*

Harris — chart of "improper" prepositions in Hellenistic Greek, p. 241; ἐνώπιον, p. 245.

ἑξῆς

▲ p. 349, *p. 276*

ADVERB

1. next, after; **S, P,** or **T**

ἔξω

▲ p. 354, *p. 279*

ADVERB USED AS A PREPOSITION WITH GENITIVE
1. outside, out (of); L [1b, 2b] [2]

ADVERB
1. (from) outside, out (of), outer, external, apart from;
    L [1a, 2a] *[1aα, γ, 1b]*

Harris — chart of "improper" prepositions in Hellenistic
Greek, p. 241; ἔξω, p. 245.

ἔξωθεν

▲ pp. 354 – 55, *pp. 279 – 80*

ADVERB USED AS A PREPOSITION WITH GENITIVE
1. from the outside, outside; L [1b, 2a] [2]

ADVERB
1. from the outside, outside, external, outward, outer;
    L [1a, 2b, 4] *[1a, bα, c]*

Harris — chart of "improper" prepositions in Hellenistic
Greek, p. 241; ἔξωθεν, pp. 245 – 46.

ἐπάν

▲ p. 358, *p. 282*

CONJUNCTION
1. when, as soon as; T

ἐπάνω

▲ p. 359, *p. 283*

ADVERB USED AS A PREPOSITION WITH GENITIVE
1. over, above, on; L [1b] *[2a]*

ADVERB
1. over, above; L [1a]

Harris — chart of "improper" prepositions in Hellenistic
Greek, p. 241; ἐπάνω, p. 246.

ἐπαύριον

▲ p. 360, *p.* 283

ADVERB

1. tomorrow, on the next day; **S, P,** or **T**

Wallace — the article used as a substantive with adverbs, pp. 231 – 33.

ἐπεί

▲ p. 360, *p.* 284

CONJUNCTION

1. when, after; **T** [1]
2. since, because, for; **G** [2]

Wallace — adverbial causal conjunctions, p. 674; ἐπεί in first class conditions, p. 692.

ἐπειδή

▲ p. 360, *p.* 284

CONJUNCTION

1. when, after; **T** [1]
2. since, then, (just) because, for; **G** [2]

Wallace — adverbial causal conjunctions, p. 674; ἐπειδή in first class conditions, p. 692.

ἐπειδήπερ

▲ p. 360, *p.* 284

CONJUNCTION

1. inasmuch, since, because (rare: Luke 1:1); **G**

Wallace — adverbial causal conjunctions, p. 674.

ἐπείπερ

▲ p. 361, *p.* 284

CONJUNCTION

1. since (rare: Rom 3:30 [*variant*]); **G**

ἔπειτα

▲ p. 361, p. 284

ADVERB
1. then, thereupon; **P** or **S** [1, 2]

ἐπέκεινα

▲ p. 361, p. 284

ADVERB USED AS A PREPOSITION WITH GENITIVE
1. beyond (rare: Acts 7:43); **L**

Harris — chart of "improper" prepositions in Hellenistic Greek, p. 241; ἐπέκεινα, p. 246.

ἐπί[13]

pp. 363 – 67, *pp. 285 – 89*

PREPOSITION WITH GENITIVE
1. on, upon, near, at, before, toward, over; **L** [1a, 2a, 3, 4a, 9a] *[I.1aα, β, γ, δ, ba]*
2. in consideration of, on the basis of, concerning; **C-E** or **G** [8] *[I.1bβ]*
3. about, over; **Gn-Sp**, **Ft-In**, or **W-Ed** [8, 9a] *[I.1ba, β, γ]*
4. in the time of, at, on, for; **T** [18a] *[I.2]*

PREPOSITION WITH DATIVE
1. on, in, above, upon, at, near, by, over, against; **L** [1b, 2b, 9b, 12a] *[II.1aα, β, γ, δ, ba]*
2. from, in, with, by manner of (rare: 2 Cor 9:6); **W-Ed** [5] *[II.1bζ]*
3. for; **M-Ed** [16] *[II.1bε]*
4. on account of, on the basis of, because of, for (sometimes with ὅς, e.g., 2 Cor 5:4; see entry for ὅς, ἥ, ὅ, below); **C-E** or **G** [6] *[II.1bγ]*
5. upon, unto, in addition to; -/+ or **P** [7] *[II.1bβ]*

---

13. The entry for ἐπί has been significantly rearranged in BDAG ('00), although the content is almost entirely identical to BAGD ('79).

6. to, on, about, indeed, for which (ἐφ' ᾧ), against; **Ft-In** or **Gn-Sp** [6c, 9b, 12a, 14a, 17] *[II.1aγ, bα, δ, 3]*

7. in the time of, at, on, for; **T** [18b] *[II.2]*

PREPOSITION WITH ACCUSATIVE

1. on, over, upon, beside, at, near, by, (up) to, toward, against, across, over, around, against, for, toward, before; **L** [1c, 4b, 9c, 10, 12b, 14bβ] *[III.1aα, β, γ, δ, ε, ζ, bα, γ, δ]*

2. upon, unto, in addition to; **P** or **NLR** [7] *[III.1bβ]*

3. to, for; **M-Ed** or **C-E** [11] *[III.1bη]*

4. inasmuch as, insofar as, to the degree that (ἐφ' ὅσον [see entries for ἐφ' ὅσον and ὅσος, ὅση, ὅσον below]); // or **G** [13] *[III.3]*

5. to, on, about, over, against; **Ft-In** or **Gn-Sp** [9c, 12b, 14b, 15] *[III.1aε, bα, γ, ε, ζ]*

6. in the time of, at, on, for; **T** [18c] *[III.2]*

7. (with various other words: πολύ, πλεῖον); **NLR** [13] *[III.3]*

Wallace — dative of destination, p. 147; Rom 5:12 and ἐφ' ᾧ, pp. 342–43; spatial diagram, p. 358; basic uses and significant passages, p. 376; independent clauses introduced by a prepositional phrase, p. 658.

Harris [pp. 137–45] — basic meaning, pp. 137–38; versatility, p. 138; important constructions using ἐπί, pp. 138–41; other notable uses of ἐπί, pp. 141–45; ἐπί in compounds, p. 145; the phrase ἐπὶ τῷ ὀνόματι, p. 232.

ἔσω

▲ p. 398, *p. 314*

ADVERB SOMETIMES USED AS A PREPOSITION

1. in, into, inside, within; **L** [1, 2]

Harris — chart of "improper" prepositions in Hellenistic Greek, p. 241; ἔσω, p. 246.

ἔτι

p. 400, *pp. 315 – 16*

ADVERB

1. yet, still; **T** [1]
2. then (a weakened inference; rare: Heb 7:11); ∴ [3] *[2c]*

εὐθέως

p. 405, *p. 320*

ADVERB

1. at once, immediately; **T** or **S-R**

εὐθύς

p. 406, *p. 321*

ADVERB

1. immediately, at once; **T** or **S-R** [1]
2. then, so then (a weakened inference; rare: Mark 1:21); ∴ [2]

ἐφ' ὅσον

▲ see ἐπί pp. 366 – 67, *p. 289*

PREPOSITION WITH ACCUSATIVE USED AS A CONJUNCTION

1. as long as; **T** [18cβ] *[III.2b]* (see also ὅσος, p. 729 [1b], *p. 586 [1]*)
2. inasmuch as, insofar as, to the degree that; (rare: Matt 25:40) // or **G** [13] *[III.3]*

Harris — ἐπί basic meaning, *pp. 137 – 38*; versatility, *p. 138*; important constructions using ἐπί, *pp. 138 – 41*; other notable uses of ἐπί, *pp. 141 – 45*; ἐπί in compounds, *p. 145*.

ἐφ' ᾧ

see ἐπί p. 365, *p. 287*; ὅς p. 727, *p. 585*

PREPOSITION WITH DATIVE USED AS A CONJUNCTION

1. for the reason that, because, for, with the result (Rom 5:12; 2 Cor 5:4); **G** or **C-E** (ἐπί [6c] *[II.1bγ]*; ὅς [1kδ] *[I.11d]*)

Wallace — see ἐπί above; Rom 5:12 and ἐφ᾽ ᾧ, pp. 342 – 43.

Harris — see esp. pp. 139 – 41; ἐπί basic meaning, pp. 137 – 38; versatility, p. 138; important constructions using ἐπί, pp. 138 – 41; other notable uses of ἐπί, pp. 141 – 45; ἐπί in compounds, p. 145.

ἕως

pp. 422 – 24, *pp. 334 – 35*

CONJUNCTION
1. until, up to, while, as long as; **T** [1a, 2a, b] *[I.1, 2]*

USED AS A PREPOSITION (OFTEN WITH GENITIVE)
1. until, up to (sometimes with relative pronouns: e.g., ὅτου, οὗ *[see also* ἕως ὅτου *and* ἕως οὗ, *below]*; or adverbs: e.g., ἄρτι, νῦν, πρωΐ); **T** [1b, 2c] *[II.1]*
2. as far as, to (sometimes with adverbs or prepositions: e.g., ἄνω, πρός); **L** [3] *[II.2]*
3. to, up to; **S** or **P** [4] *[II.3]*
4. as many as, up to, unto; **Gn-Sp** or **Ft-In** [5] *[II.4]*

Wallace — genitive after certain prepositions, p. 136; subjunctive in indefinite temporal clauses, p. 479; common subordinating conjunctions, p. 669; adverbial temporal conjunctions, p. 677.

Harris — chart of "improper" prepositions in Hellenistic Greek, p. 241; ἕως, pp. 246 – 47; notable uses of selected "improper" prepositions: ἕως οὗ, pp. 262 – 63.

ἕως ὅτου

see ἕως p. 423, *p. 335*

PREPOSITION WITH GENITIVE USED AS A CONJUNCTION
1. until; **T** [1bבּ, 2c] *[II.1β]*

Wallace — adverbial/conjunctive uses of relative pronouns, p. 343.

Harris — ἕως, pp. 246 – 47.

ἕως οὗ

see ἕως p. 423, *p. 335*; ὅς p. 727, *p. 585*

PREPOSITION WITH GENITIVE USED AS A CONJUNCTION
1. until, before; **T** (ἕως [1bβℵ, 2c] *[II.1bα, γ]*; ὅς [1kζ] *[I.11f]*)

Harris — ἕως, pp. 246 – 47; notable uses of selected "improper" prepositions: ἕως οὗ, pp. 262 – 63.

ἤ

pp. 432 – 33, *pp. 342 – 43*

PARTICLE USED AS A CONJUNCTION
1. or, nor; **Alt** [1a, c]
2. or; **Alt, Adv, S,** or **Ft-In** [1dα, β, δ]
3. than; **//, Adv,** or **-/+** [2a, b]
4. (other/else) than (rare: Acts 24:21); **C?-E** [2c]
5. before (with πρίν, rare; Matt 1:18); **T** [2d]

Wallace — to indicate comparison, pp. 297, 299; adverbial, temporal use of the infinitive, pp. 596, 609; common Greek coordinating conjunctions, pp. 658, 669; logical disjunctive (alternative) conjunctions, p. 672.

ἤ ... ἤ

see ἤ p. 432, *p. 342*

CONJUNCTION COMBINED WITH ANOTHER CONJUNCTION
1. either/whether ... or; **Alt** [1b, dγ]

Wallace — logical correlative (paired) conjunctions, p. 672.

ἥ

Relative pronoun; see ὅς *below.*

ἡνίκα

▲ p. 439, *p. 348*

PARTICLE USED AS A CONJUNCTION
1. whenever, when, as soon as, every time that (sometimes used with ἄν or ἐάν; see entries; rare: 2 Cor 3:16); **T**

ἤπερ

see ἤ p. 433, *p. 343*

PARTICLE
1. (combined with μᾶλλον) than; -/+ [2eβ]

ἥτις

Relative pronoun; see ὅστις *below.*

ἤτοι ... ἤ

see ἤ p. 432, *p. 342*

PARTICLE COMBINED WITH A CONJUNCTION
1. either ... or (rare: Rom 6:16); **Alt** [1b]

Wallace — logical correlative (paired) conjunctions, p. 672.

ἵνα

pp. 475 – 77, *pp. 376 – 78*

CONJUNCTION
1. in order that, for this purpose, so that, with the result that; **M-Ed** or **C-E** [1, 2f, g, h, 3, 4] *[I, II.2, III, IV]*
2. that; **Ft-In** or **Gn-Sp** [2a, b, c, d, e, 4] *[II.1, IV]*

Wallace — ἵνα plus subjunctive, pp. 471 – 77; subjunctive equivalents, p. 571; syntactical function of dependent clauses using ἵνα, including the substantival subject, predicate nominative, direct object, and apposition, p. 661, and the adjectival complementary, purpose, and result, pp. 664 – 65; use of conjunctions in exegesis, pp. 668 – 69; adverbial purpose and result conjunctions, pp. 676 – 77; substantival content and epexegetical conjunctions, p. 678.

κἀγώ

p. 487, *p.* 386

COMPOUND FORMED BY CRASIS (καί + ἐγώ)
1. and I, I also, I too, for my part; **S, P, S-R,** ∴,
   or -/+ [1, 3a, b]
2. but I; **Adv, Alt,** or -/+ [2]
3. if I (rare: Matt 26:15); **C?-E** [3b, 5 (BDAG only)]

See also entry for καί *below. Can be combined with other
morphological forms of* ἐγώ.

καθά

▲ p. 487, *p.* 386

CONJUNCTION OR ADVERB
1. just as; //

καθάπερ

▲ p. 488, *p.* 387

CONJUNCTION OR ADVERB
1. just as; //

Wallace — adverbial comparative (manner) conjunctions,
p. 675.

καθό

▲ p. 493, *p.* 390

ADVERB
1. as; // [1]
2. in so far as, to the degree that; **Ft-In, Gn-Sp,** or **W-Ed** [2]

καθότι

▲ p. 493, *p.* 391

CONJUNCTION
1. as, to the degree that; **Ft-In, Gn-Sp,** or **W-Ed** [1]
2. because, in view of the fact that; **G** [2]

καθώς

pp. 493–94, *p. 391*

ADVERB

1. just as, as (sometimes combined with, e.g., καί, ὁμοίως, οὕτως); // [1]
2. as, to the degree that, that, how; **Ft-In, Gn-Sp,** or **W-Ed** [2, 5]
3. since, insofar as; **G** [3]
4. as; **T** [4]

Wallace — dependent, adverbial clauses of comparison, pp. 662–63; common Greek subordinating conjunctions, p. 669; adverbial causal and comparative conjunctions, pp. 674–75.

καί[14]

pp. 494–96, *pp. 391–93*

CONJUNCTION

1. and, then; **S** or **P** [1aα, β, δ, ε, bα, ε, ζ, ι, e, f] *[I.1a, b, d, e, 2a, e, f, i, 5, 6]*
2. and, and in general, and all the rest, and especially, and so, that is, namely; **Gn-Sp** or **Ft-In** [1aγ, ε, bβ, γ, ζ, c] *[I.1c, e, 2b, c, f, 3]*
3. and; **W-Ed** or **G** [1aε] *[I.1e]*
4. and, and then, so; ∴ , **C-E, C?-E,** or **S-R** [1aε, bβ, ζ, θ] *[I.1e, 2b, f, h]*

---

14. Καί is the most frequent of Greek particles by far (9018 occurrences in the NT alone), partly due to the fact that it is used in circumstances not strictly "normal" for a conjunction. BDAG ('00) states it is used with "vivacious versatility," often "as a connective where more discriminating usage would call for other particles" (494). Its use is not unlike our own use of the English "and." Much of the semantic diversity of καί results from the bilingualism of the NT writers and the influence of biblical Hebrew, as well as of the Greek of the Septuagint. Because of the flexibility of καί, it can be used to signal a wide variety of logical relationships. The specific semantic (or logical) relationship signaled in each instance must be derived from the context.

5. then (or left untranslated); **T** or **C?-E** [1bδ] *[I.2d]*
6. and, and yet, and in spite of that, nevertheless, although; **Adv** [1bη, ι, f] *[I.2g, i, 6]*

CONJUNCTION USED AS AN ADVERB
1. also, even, indeed; **S, P, Gn-Sp, Ft-In,** or **NLR** [2] *[II]*
2. thus also, in the same way, so also (often combined with other words, e.g., καθάπερ, ὥσπερ, ὁμοίως, etc., but καί can introduce on its own the second member of a comparison); // [2c] *[II.3]*
3. also, then; **C?-E** [2e] *[II.5]*

Wallace — καί and genitive after certain nouns, "between," p. 135; the article with multiple substantives connected by καί (Granville Sharp Rule and related constructions), pp. 270 – 90; 2 Tim 3:16 and καί, pp. 313 – 14; Eph 2:8 and καί, pp. 334 – 35; conditional imperative, pp. 489 – 92; classification of independent clauses, pp. 657 – 58; dependent, adverbial clauses of concession, p. 663; introduction to conjunctions, p. 667; conjunctions in exegesis, common Greek coordinating conjunctions, and logical categories, pp. 668 – 73.

καί ... καί

see καί p. 495, *p. 393*

CONJUNCTION COMBINED WITH ANOTHER CONJUNCTION
1. both ... and, not only ... but also; **S** or **P** [1f] *[I.6]*
2. although ... yet, even though ... nevertheless; **Adv** [1f] *[I.6]*

Wallace — independent clauses introduced by a coordinating conjunction, p. 658; logical correlative (paired) conjunctions, p. 672.

καίπερ

▲ p. 497, *p. 394*

CONJUNCTION
1. although, though, even though (rare: Phil 3:4); **Adv**

Wallace — clauses (dependent), syntactical function, adverbial clause, concession, p. 663.

καίτοι

▲ see καί p. 496, καίτοι *p. 396*

PARTICLE

1. and yet, yet, on the other hand, although (rare: Heb 4:3); **Adv** [2iδ] (see also *BAGD, p. 396*)

καίτοιγε (καίτοι γε, καί τοι γε)

▲ see καί p. 496, καίτοιγε *p. 396*

PARTICLE

1. although (rare: John 4:2); **Adv** [2iδ] (see also *BAGD, p. 396*)

Wallace — clauses (dependent), syntactical function, adverbial clause, concession, p. 663.

κἀκεῖ

▲ p. 499, *p. 396*

ADVERB FORMED BY CRASIS (καί + ἐκεῖ)

1. and there, there also; **S, P,** or **C-E** 1

See also entry for καί above.

κἀκεῖθεν

▲ p. 499, *p. 396*

ADVERB FORMED BY CRASIS (καί + ἐκεῖθεν)

1. and from there; **S** or **P** [1]
2. and then; **S, P,** or **T** [2]

See also entry for καί above.

κἀκεῖνος

▲ p. 500, *p. 396*

CONJUNCTION FORMED BY CRASIS (καί + ἐκεῖνος)

1. and that (one, thing), that (one, thing) also, and he (she, it, that, they, etc.); **S, P, S-R, C-E,** or **C?-E** [1, 2]

See also entry for καί *above.*

κἀμέ

See κἀγώ *above.*

κἀμοί

See κἀγώ *above.*

κἄν

▲ p. 507, *p. 402*

PARTICLE FORMED BY CRASIS (καί + ἐάν)

1. and if; **S, P,** or **C?-E** [1]
2. even if, even though; **Adv** or **C?-E** [2]
3. (even) if only, even at least; **NLR** [3]

See also entry for ἐάν *above.*

κατά

pp. 511 – 13, *pp. 405 – 8*

PREPOSITION WITH GENITIVE

1. down from, on, into, throughout, down upon, toward, against; **L,**[15] **Gn-Sp,** or **Ft-In** [A] *[I]*

---

15. This Locative function of κατά with the genitive demonstrates how the "logically orienting information" provided may be either spatial *or* relational: e.g., "Throw a rock *against* the wall" (spatial, [A1] *[I.1]*), and "Hold a grudge *against* an enemy" (relational [A2] *[I.2]*). In this sense, this relationship may be more broadly (i.e., less specifically) labeled Gn-Sp or Ft-In. See further "Logical Relationships between Clauses" in the Introduction above.

Preposition with accusative

1. along, over, through, in, upon, toward, to, up to, by; L [B1] [II.1]
2. at, on, during, in, toward, about; T [B2] [II.2]
3. at a time, in detail, by; Gn-Sp or Ft-In [B3] [II.3]
4. for the purpose of, for, to; M-Ed [B4] [II.4]
5. according to, in accordance with, in conformity with, in (such and such) a manner; W-Ed, Gn-Sp, or Ft-In [B5a, bβ, 6] [II.5a, bβ, 6]
6. in accordance with, on the basis of, on account of, because of; G or C-E [B5aδ] [II.5aδ]
7. in accordance with, just as, similarly; // or G [B5aδ, ba] [II.5aδ, ba]
8. (functioning, with its object, like an adjective, possessive pronoun, or genitive noun; see, e.g., Rom 11:21: "the natural branches"); NLR [B7] [II.7]

Wallace — spatial diagram, p. 358; basic uses and significant passages, pp. 376 – 77; independent clauses introduced by a prepositional phrase, p. 658.

Harris [pp. 147 – 60] — basic meaning, p. 147; phrases involving κατά, pp. 147 – 52; κατά denoting correspondence or conformity, pp. 152 – 54; κατά denoting opposition, pp. 154 – 55; distributive κατά, pp. 155 – 57; some ambiguous examples, pp. 157 – 60; κατά in compounds, p. 160.

κατέναντι

▲ pp. 530 – 31, *p.* 421

Adverb

1. opposite, before; L [2a] [1]

Used as a preposition with genitive

1. opposite, in the sight of, before; L [1, 2b] [2]

Harris — chart of "improper" prepositions in Hellenistic Greek, pp. 240 – 41; κατέναντι, p. 247.

κατενώπιον

▲ p. 531, *p. 421*

ADVERB USED AS A PREPOSITION WITH GENITIVE

1. before, opposite, in the presence of, in front of;
   L [1, 2] [a, b]

Harris — chart of "improper" prepositions in Hellenistic Greek, pp. 240 – 41; κατενώπιον, p. 247.

κάτω

▲ p. 535, *p. 425*

ADVERB

1. below, downwards, down; L or NLR [1, 2] [a, b]

κυκλόθεν

▲ p. 574, *p. 456*

ADVERB

1. around, all around, from all sides; L or NLR [1]

USED AS A PREPOSITION WITH GENITIVE

1. around, all around, from all sides; L or NLR [2]

Harris — chart of "improper" prepositions in Hellenistic Greek, pp. 240 – 41; κυκλόθεν, p. 247.

κύκλῳ

▲ p. 574, *pp. 456 – 57*

DATIVE OF PLACE, FIXED AS AN ADVERB

1. around; L or NLR [1, 2, 3] [1]

USED AS A PREPOSITION WITH GENITIVE

1. around; L or NLR [1] [2]

Harris — ἀνὰ μέσον and ὁ θρόνος in Revelation, pp. 46 – 47; chart of "improper" prepositions in Hellenistic Greek, p. 242; κύκλῳ, p. 247.

μακράν

▲ p. 612, *p*. 487

ACCUSATIVE OF EXTENT USED AS AN ADVERB
1. far (away); **L** or **NLR** [1a]

ACCUSATIVE OF EXTENT USED AS A PREPOSITION
1. far away; **L** [1b] *[2]*

Wallace — adverbial accusatives (accusative of manner), p. 201.

μᾶλλον

▲ pp. 613 – 14, *p*. 489

COMPARATIVE ADVERB
1. rather, instead (often with δέ or ἀλλά, or complementing ἤ); **Alt** or -/+ [3aα, b, c]
2. rather, but rather, or rather (with δέ); **P, Gn-Sp,** or **Ft-In** [3d]
3. more, rather, all the more; **NLR** [1, 2]

Wallace — dative of measure/degree of difference, p. 167.

μέν

pp. 629 – 30, *pp*. 502 – 3

PARTICLE
1. to be sure ... but, on the one hand ... on the other hand; **S, P, Adv, Alt,** or +/- [1, 2a, b, c, d, e][16]

The particle μέν often introduces a concessive clause, followed by another clause with other particles or conjunctions, including ἀλλά, δέ, and πλήν (see entries above and below).

Wallace — the article used as a third-personal or alternative-personal pronoun with μέν ... δέ, pp. 211 – 13; independent clauses introduced by a coordinating

---

16. The semantic-relational uses of μέν described in sections [1, 2a, b] are too intermingled in BDAG/BAGD to distinguish easily. Thus the exegete must defer to context in individual cases to determine the semantic relationship.

conjunction, p. 658; logical correlative (paired) conjunctions, p. 672. (Also see δέ.)

μέν ... ἀλλά

see μέν p. 630, *p. 502*

PARTICLE COMBINED WITH A CONJUNCTION
1. to be sure ... but; **Adv** or **Alt** [1aβ]

Wallace — see page references listed in the entry for μέν above; see also the entry for ἀλλά above.

μέν ... δέ[17]

see μέν pp. 629 – 30, *pp. 502 – 3*

PARTICLE COMBINED WITH A CONJUNCTION
1. to be sure ... but, indeed ... but, if/for indeed ... but (if), on the one hand ... but on the other hand; **Adv** or **Alt** [1aα][18]
2. on the one hand ... and on the other hand; **S** [1c]

Wallace — see page references listed in the entry for μέν above; see also the entry for δέ above.

μέν ... πλήν

see μέν p. 630, *p. 502*

PARTICLE COMBINED WITH A CONJUNCTION
1. indeed ... but/nevertheless; **Adv** or **Alt** [1aγ]

Wallace — see page references listed in the entry for μέν above; see also the entry for πλήν below.

---

17. This combination may also connect two or more εἰ/ἐάν clauses (see 1aα). In the combination μέν ... δέ, μέν may not always have a strong concessive sense, so that it need not always be translated (see 1b). Sometimes μέν ... δέ separates thoughts in a Series relationship as well (see 1c).

18. In combination with εἰ or other conjunctions/particles, μέν ... δέ may introduce an Alt or Adv relationship in the larger context of another relationship, e.g., C?-E (see, e.g., Acts 19:38 – 39; Rom 2:25).

μενοῦν

▲ p. 630, *p. 503*

COMBINED PARTICLE (μέν + οὖν)

1. rather, on the contrary; **Adv, Alt,** or **S-R**

μενοῦνγε

▲ see μενοῦν p. 630, *p. 503*

COMBINED PARTICLE (μενοῦν + γέ)

1. rather, on the contrary, indeed; **Adv, Alt, S-R,** or **P**

Wallace — logical emphatic conjunctions, p. 673.

μέντοι

▲ p. 630, *p. 503*

PARTICLE USED AS A CONJUNCTION

1. though, to be sure, indeed, yet, despite that, but;
   Adv or **Alt** [2]

In combination with ὅμως, *see entry for* ὅμως *below.*

Wallace — logical emphatic conjunctions, p. 673.

μέσον

▲ see μέσος pp. 634 – 35, *pp. 507 – 8*

NEUTER ADJECTIVE, SOMETIMES USED AS AN ADVERB OR
PREPOSITION WITH GENITIVE

1. in the midst, in the middle/center, among; **L** [1c] *[3]*

Harris — chart of "improper" prepositions in Hellenistic
Greek, p. 242; μέσον, pp. 247 – 48.

μετά

pp. 636 – 38, *pp. 508 – 10*

PREPOSITION WITH GENITIVE

1. with, among, in company with someone; **L** [A1, 2]
   [A.I, II]

2. with; **Gn-Sp** [A2αγ, c, 3] *[A.II.1c, III]*
3. with, in, accompanied by; **W-Ed** [A3] *[A.III]*

PREPOSITION WITH ACCUSATIVE
1. after, behind; **L** [B1] *[B.I]*
2. after; **T** [B2] *[B.II]*

See also μετὰ τό + inf., *below*

Wallace — dative of manner, p. 161; μετά with conceptual antecedent/postcedent pronouns, p. 333; basic uses and significant passages, and relationship to σύν, pp. 377 – 78; adverbial infinitive of time, pp. 594 – 95; independent clauses introduced by a prepositional phrase, p. 658.

Harris [pp. 161 – 70] — original meaning and NT use, p. 161; μετά with accusative ("after"), pp. 161 – 63; μετά with genitive, pp. 163 – 68; εἶναι μετά denoting "presence with," pp. 168 – 70; μετά in compounds, p. 170.

μετὰ τό + inf.

see μετά p. 638, *p. 510*

PREPOSITION WITH ACCUSATIVE ARTICULAR INFINITIVE
1. after; **T** [B2d] *[B.II.4]*

Wallace — infinitive, adverbial uses, time, pp. 594 – 95; articular infinitives, p. 611.

μεταξύ

▲ p. 641, *pp. 512 – 13*

ADVERB
1. between, in the middle; **L** [1aα] *[1a]*
2. meanwhile, between, afterward, next, following; **T** [1b] *[1b]*

USED AS A PREPOSITION WITH GENITIVE
1. in the middle of, between; **L** [1aβ] *[2a]*
2. between, among; **W-Ed** or **Gn-Sp** [2] *[2b]*

Wallace — genitive after certain nouns, p. 135.

Harris — chart of "improper" prepositions in Hellenistic Greek, p. 242; μεταξύ, p. 248.

μετέπειτα
▲ p. 642, *p. 514*

ADVERB
1. afterwards (rare: Heb 12:17); T

μέχρι(ς)
▲ p. 644, *p. 515*

CONJUNCTION USED AS A PREPOSITION WITH GENITIVE
1. as far as; L [1] *[1a]*
2. until, to; T [2a] *[1b]*
3. to the point of (rare: Phil 2:8); **Gn-Sp** [3] *[1c]*

CONJUNCTION
1. until (also with relative pronoun οὗ, see next entry); T [2b] *[2]*

See also entry for ὅς *below.*

Wallace — temporal adverbs (or improper prepositions) used with the subjunctive, p. 479.

Harris — chart of "improper" prepositions in Hellenistic Greek, p. 242; μέχρις, p. 248.

μέχρις οὗ
▲ see μέχρι(ς) p. 644, *p. 515*; cf. ὅς p. 727, *p. 585*

CONJUNCTION
1. until (rare: Mark 13:30); T [2b] *[2]* (cf. ὅς [1kζ] *[I.11f]*)

Wallace — temporal adverbs (or improper prepositions) used with the subjunctive, p. 479.

Harris — chart of "improper" prepositions in Hellenistic Greek, p. 242; μέχρις, p. 248.

μή

pp. 644 – 46, *pp. 515 – 17*

NEGATIVE PARTICLE SOMETIMES USED AS A MARKER OF CONJUNCTION

1. not; -/+ or **Adv** [1, 2, 4] [A, B, D]
2. lest (= so that ... not), that ... (no/not); **C-E** or **Gn-Sp** [2] [B]
3. (in direct questions expecting a negative answer); **Q-A** [3] [C]

See also entry for εἰ *above.*

Wallace — emphatic negation subjunctive, pp. 468 – 69; prohibitive subjunctive, p. 469; subjunctive with verbs of fearing, etc., p. 477; voluntative optative, pp. 481 – 83; verbal moods: prohibition, p. 487; request, pp. 487 – 88; conditional imperative, pp. 489 – 90; subjunctive equivalents in future tense, p. 571; common subordinating conjunctions, p. 669; emphatic conjunctions, p. 673; volitional clauses: prohibitions with aorist + μή, pp. 723 – 24; present imperative + μή, p. 724.

μηδέ

p. 647, *pp. 517 – 18*

NEGATIVE DISJUNCTIVE PARTICLE

1. and not, but not, nor; **S, P,** or **Alt** [1a, b]
2. then, neither (in the apodosis of a conditional sentence; rare: 2 Thess 3:10); **C?-E** [1c]
3. not even; **Gn-Sp** or **NLR** [2]

Wallace — logical ascensive conjunctions, pp. 670 – 71.

μηκέτι

▲ p. 647, *p. 518*

ADVERB

1. no longer, not from now on; -/+ or **NLR**

μήποτε

▲ pp. 648 – 49, *p. 519*

CONJUNCTION

1. so that … not, lest, otherwise; **M-Ed** [2]
2. whether perhaps (in direct and indirect questions); **Gn-Sp** [3]
3. never (rare: Heb 9:17), perhaps, probably; **NLR** [1, 4]

Wallace — common Greek subordinating conjunctions in subjunctive, p. 669; adverbial purpose conjunctions, p. 676.

μήτε

▲ p. 649, *pp. 519 – 20*

NEGATIVE PARTICLE

1. and not, neither, nor, either, or (often paired with other negative particles [e.g., μή, μήτε]); **S, P,** or **Alt**

Wallace — correlative conjunctions (paired conjunctions), p. 672.

ναί

▲ p. 665, *pp. 532 – 33*

PARTICLE OF AFFIRMATION

1. yes, indeed; **Q-A** or **S-R** [a, b] *[1, 2]*
2. yes, indeed; **P** or **Ft-In** [c] *[3]*

Wallace — emphatic conjunctions, p. 673.

νή

▲ p. 670, *p. 537*

PARTICLE

1. by (rare: 1 Cor 15:31); **Ft-In** or **NLR**

Wallace — emphatic conjunctions, p. 673.

ὅ

Relative pronoun; see ὅς *below.*

ὅ τι

Relative pronoun; see ὅστις below.

ὅδε, ἥδε, τόδε

▲ pp. 689 – 90, p. 553

DEMONSTRATIVE PRONOUN
1. this; **Gn-Sp** or **NLR** [1a] *[1]*

Wallace — pronouns, demonstrative pronouns, ὅδε, p. 328; lexico-syntactic categories: major terms, pp. 353 – 54.

ὅθεν

▲ pp. 692 – 93, p. 555

ADVERB
1. from where, whence, from which; **L** [1a] *[1]*
2. from which fact (rare: 1 John 2:18), for which reason, so, therefore; ∴ or **C-E** [1b, 2] *[2, 3]*

Wallace — adverbial local (sphere) conjunctions, p. 676.

οἷος, οἵα, οἷον

▲ p. 701, p. 562

RELATIVE PRONOUN
1. of what sort, such (often complementing τοιοῦτος); //, **Ft-In, Gn-Sp,** or **NLR**

See also entry for τοιοῦτος, τοιαύτη, τοιοῦτον below.

Wallace — clauses, classification of dependent clauses, structure, p. 659.

ὁμοίως

pp. 707 – 8, pp. 567 – 68

ADVERB
1. likewise, so, similarly, in the same way (sometimes paired with κάθως); **S, P, //, W-Ed,** or **NLR**

ὅμως

▲ p. 710, *p. 569*

ADVERSATIVE PARTICLE[19]

1. all the same, yet, nevertheless (sometimes strengthened with μέντοι; e.g., John 12:42); **Adv**
2. equally, also, likewise (possibly, e.g., Gal 3:15); //

ὃν τρόπον

▲ see τρόπος, ου, ὁ, pp. 1016 – 17, *p. 827*

RELATIVE PRONOUN WITH NOUN USED AS A CONJUNCTION

1. in the manner in which, just as (rare: Matt 23:37);
   // [1]

May be correlated with οὕτω(ς); *see entry for* οὕτω(ς) *below.*

ὄπισθεν

▲ pp. 715 – 16, *pp. 574 – 75*

ADVERB

1. from behind, to the rear, after; **L** or **NLR** [1a, 2] *[1a, b]*

USED AS A PREPOSITION WITH GENITIVE

1. from behind, to the rear, after; **L** [1bα] *[2a]*

Harris — chart of "improper" prepositions in Hellenistic Greek, p. 242; ὄπισθεν, p. 248.

ὀπίσω

▲ p. 716, *p. 575*

ADVERB

1. behind, back; **L** or **NLR** [1a] *[1]*

USED AS A PREPOSITION WITH GENITIVE

1. behind, after; **L** [1b, 2a] *[2a]*
2. after; **T** [2b]

Harris — chart of "improper" prepositions in Hellenistic Greek, p. 242; ὀπίσω, p. 248.

---

19. BAGD ('79) lists this word as an adverb.

ὁποῖος, ὁποία, ὁποῖον

▲ pp. 716–17, p. 575

CORRELATIVE PRONOUN

1. of what sort, as (sometimes paired with τοιοῦτος); //,
   Ft-In, Gn-Sp, or **NLR**

ὁπότε

▲ p. 717, p. 576

PARTICLE

1. when; **T**

ὅπου

▲ p. 717, p. 576

PARTICLE

1. where, wherever (with ἄν); **L** [1aα, γ, δ, bα, β; 2] *[1aα, γ, δ, bα, β; 2a]*
2. whenever (sometimes used with ἄν or ἐάν; see entries above); **T** [1aβ, δ]
3. where (introducing the protasis of a conditional sentence; rare: Heb 9:16); **C?-E** [2] *[2a]*
4. insofar as, since (rare: 1 Cor 3:3); **G** [3] *[2b]*

Wallace — dependent relative clauses, p. 659; dependent location clauses, p. 664; adverbial local (sphere) conjunctions, p. 676.

ὅπως

p. 718, *pp.* 576–77

ADVERB

1. how, that; **Gn-Sp** [1]

CONJUNCTION

1. in order that, so that (sometimes negated by μή); **M-Ed** or **C-E** [2a]
2. that; **Ft-In** or **Gn-Sp** [2b]

Wallace — common Greek subordinating conjunctions in the subjunctive mood, p. 669; adverbial purpose conjunctions, p. 676; adverbial result conjunctions, p. 677.

ὅς, ἥ, ὅ
pp. 725 – 27, *pp.* 583 – 85

RELATIVE PRONOUN
1. who, that, which, what; **Ft-In, Gn-Sp, S, P, C-E**, or **G** [1a, b, c, d, e, f, g, h, i] *[I.1, 2, 3, 4, 5, 6, 7, 8, 9][20]*
2. that, so that; (rare: 1 Cor 2:16) **C-E** or **G** [1h] *[I.8]*

GENITIVE USED AS A MARKER OF LOCATION
See entry for οὗ *below.*

COMBINED WITH OTHER PARTICLES AND PREPOSITIONS
1. ἄν, ἐάν, γέ, καί (see each individual entry for semantic functions) [1jα, β, δ] *[I.10a, b, d]*
2. τίς (see entry for ὅστις, ἥτις, ὅ τι below)
3. ἀντί — because, therefore (see also entry for ἀνθ᾽ ὧν above); **G, C-E**, or ∴ [1kα] *[I.11a]*
4. εἰς — to this end (rare: 2 Thess 1:11); **Ft-In** [1kβ] *[I.11b]*
5. ἐν — under which circumstances (but cf. the entry for ἐν ᾧ above); **S-R, T,** or **P**[1kγ] *[I.11c]*
6. ἐπί — for the reason that, because, for, for which, on which (see also entries for ἐπί and ἐφ᾽ ᾧ above); **G** or **C-E** [1kδ] *[I.11d]*
7. χάριν — therefore (see also entries for οὗ χάριν and χάριν below; rare: Luke 7:47); ∴ [1kε] *[I.11e]*
8. ἀπό — from the time when; since; as soon as, after, until (see entries for ἀφ᾽ ἧς and ἀφ᾽ οὗ above); **T** [1kζ] *[I.11f]*
9. ἄχρι — until (see also entry for ἄχρι[ς] above); **T** [1kζ] *[I.11f]*

---

20. The relative pronoun can function in possibly every logical relationship. Context will decide.

10. ἕως — until (see also entries for ἕως and ἕως οὗ above);
    T [1kζ] [I.11f]

11. μέχρις — until (see also entries for μέχρι(ς) and μέχρις
    οὗ above); T [1kζ] [I.11f]

Wallace — the relative pronoun represented by the article,
p. 213; relative pronouns, pp. 335 – 45; subjunctive in
indefinite relative clauses, pp. 478 – 80; classification of
dependent clauses, p. 659; subjective uses of dependent
clauses, p. 661; adverbial, manner/means uses of dependent clauses, p. 664; implicit conditional sentences using
a relative clause, p. 688.

ὁσάκις

▲ p. 728, *p. 585*; see also ἄν p. 57, *p. 49*; ἐάν p. 268, *p. 211*

ADVERB

1. as often as (with ἄν or ἐάν); T (ἄν [I.cγ] *[3c]*; ἐάν [3]
   [II])

ὅσος, ὅση, ὅσον

p. 729, *p. 586*

CORRELATIVE PRONOUN

1. as great as, as far as, as long as; // [1a] [1]
2. as long as (see also entries for ἐπί and ἐφ᾽ ὅσον above);
   T [1b] *[2]*
3. how much, how many, as much as, as many as; // [2]
4. all, all that, all who, as many as, whoever, whatever
   (sometimes with [ἅ]πάντες, or ἀν/ἐάν); **Gn-Sp, C?-E,**
   or **Ft-In** [2]

COMBINED WITH OTHER WORDS IN PHRASES OF
COMPARISON

1. as much as ... so much the more (ὅσον ... μᾶλλον
   περισσότερον; Mark 7:36); // or **Adv** [3]
2. as much as, inasmuch as, to the degree that, just as
   (καθ᾽ ὅσον; Heb 3:3; 7:20; 9:27); // [3]

See entry for τοσοῦτος, τοσαύτη, τοσοῦτον *below.*

Wallace — classification of dependent clauses, p. 659; adverbial, dependent clauses of comparison, p. 662; semantic converse of conditional sentences, pp. 685 – 86.

ὅστις, ἥτις, ὅ τι

pp. 729 – 30, *pp.* 586 – 87

INDEFINITE RELATIVE PRONOUN

1. whoever, whatever, everyone who, who; **Ft In, Gn-Sp, C?-E, C-E,** or **G**[21] [1, 2, 3]
2. why? what, (ὅ τι or ὅτι); **Gn-Sp** or **Q-A** [4]
3. when, once (ἕως ὅτου); **T** [6]

Wallace — relative pronouns, pp. 335 – 36; ὅστις general use, pp. 343 – 45; subjunctive in indefinite relative clauses, pp. 478 – 79; dependent, adverbial clauses, pp. 662 – 64; relative clauses and conditional ideas, p. 688.

ὅταν

pp. 730 – 31, *pp.* 587 – 88

TEMPORAL PARTICLE

1. at the time that, whenever, when, as often as, every time that; **T** or **C?-E** [1] *[1, 2]*

Wallace — subjunctive in the indefinite temporal clause, p. 479; common Greek subordinating conjunctions in subjunctive, p. 669; adverbial temporal conjunctions, p. 677.

ὅτε

p. 731, *p.* 588

TEMPORAL PARTICLE

1. when, while, as long as; **T** [1a, 2] *[1]*
2. when, in which; **Gn-Sp** or **Ft-In** [1b] *[2]*

---

21. Relative pronouns function in possibly every logical relationship. Context will decide.

Wallace — relative, dependent clauses, p. 659; dependent, adverbial clauses of time, p. 665; common Greek subordinating conjunctions, p. 669; adverbial temporal conjunctions, p. 677.

ὅτι

pp. 731 – 32, *pp. 588 – 89*

CONJUNCTION

1. that; **Ft-In** or **Gn-Sp** [1, 2, 3, 5a, b] *[1a, b, c, dα, β, 2]*
2. because, since, for; **G** [4] *[3]*
3. so that, in order that (rare: John 7:35); **M-Ed** or **C-E** [5c] *[1dγ]*

Wallace — the indicative with ὅτι (including direct and indirect discourse), pp. 453 – 61; present retained in indirect discourse, pp. 537 – 38; imperfect retained in indirect discourse, pp. 552 – 53; substantival and adjectival dependent clauses, pp. 660 – 62; common Greek subordinating conjunctions, p. 669; adverbial causal conjunctions, p. 674; adverbial result conjunctions, p. 677; substantival content conjunctions, p. 678.

οὗ

pp. 732 – 33, *pp. 589 – 90*

ADVERB

1. where, in, at, on which, to which; **L** [1] *[1a, 2]*

See also entry for οὗ χάριν *below.*

CONJUNCTION

1. where (introducing the protasis of a conditional sentence); **C? E** [2] *[1b]*

Wallace — dependent, adverbial clauses of location, p. 664; adverbial local (sphere) conjunctions, p. 676.

οὐ

pp. 733 – 34, *pp. 590 – 91*

NEGATIVE ADVERB

1. not; -/+ [2αγ, bβ, f] [2c, 3b, 7]
2. (in direct quotations expecting a positive answer);
   Q-A [3a] *[4a]*

Wallace — correlative conjunctions (paired conjunctions),
p. 672.

οὗ χάριν

see ὅς p. 727, *p. 585*; χάριν pp. 1078 – 79, *p. 877*

CONJUNCTION

1. for this reason, therefore; ∴ (ὅς [1κε] *[I.11e]*; χάριν
   [b] *[2]*)

Harris — chart of "improper" prepositions in Hellenistic
Greek, p. 242; χάριν, p. 250.

οὐδέ

pp. 734 – 35, *p. 591*

CONJUNCTION

1. and not, nor; **Alt, S, P,** or **NLR** [1]
2. also not, not either, neither, not even; **NLR** [2, 3]

Wallace — common Greek coordinating conjunctions,
p. 669.

οὐκέτι

p. 736, *p. 592*

ADVERB

1. no longer (following an εἰ clause); **C?-E** [2]

Wallace — temporal conjunctions, p. 677.

οὐκοῦν

▲ p. 736, *p. 592*

ADVERB

1. so then (rare: John 18:37); ∴, **C-E,** and/or **Q-A** [2]

οὖν

pp. 736 – 37, *pp.* 592 – 93

CONJUNCTION

1. therefore, so, consequently, accordingly, then; ∴ or **C-E** [1]
2. so, now, then, in turn (usually in historical narrative); **P, C-E,** or **S-R** [2a, b, c]
3. certainly, really, to be sure, indeed, of course; **Ft-In** or **NLR** [3]
4. but, however (rare: Rom 10:14); **Adv** or **S-R** [4][22]
5. (combined with ἄρα; see also entry above) therefore, then, so then; **P** or ∴ [2d] *[5]*

Wallace — independent clauses introduced by coordinating, transitional conjunction, p. 658; common Greek coordinating conjunctions, p. 669.

οὔτε (... οὔτε)

▲ p. 740, *p.* 596

ADVERB

1. and not, neither ... nor; **S, P,** or **Alt**

Wallace — logical correlative conjunctions, p. 672.

οὕτω(ς)

pp. 741 – 42, *pp.* 597 – 98

ADVERB

1. in this manner, thus (referring to what precedes); **W-Ed** or **NLR** [1b]
2. as follows, in this way (referring to what follows); **Gn-Sp** or **W-Ed** [2]
3. therefore, thus, so, hence; ∴ [1b]

---

22. BDAG ('00) / BAGD ('79) describe this relationship as having a "slightly adversative sense" (737, 593). Both 3. and 4. in BDAG ('00) /BAGD ('79) are debatable classifications of the particle οὖν.

4. just as ... so (also); // [1a, 2]

   a. καθάπερ ... οὕτως

   b. καθώς ... οὕτως

   c. ὡς ... οὕτως

   d. ὥσπερ ... οὕτως

   e. καθ' ὅσον ... οὕτως

   f. ὃν τρόπον ... οὕτως

Wallace — adverbial comparative conjunctions (manner), p. 675

οὐχί

p. 742, *p.* 598

NEGATIVE ADVERB

1. not; -/+ [1, 2]

ὀψέ

▲ p. 746, *p.* 601

ADVERB

1. late, in the evening; **T** or **NLR** [2]

USED AS A PREPOSITION WITH GENITIVE

1. after, later; **T** [3]

Wallace — genitive after certain prepositions, p. 136.

Harris — chart of "improper" prepositions in Hellenistic Greek, p. 242; ὀψέ, pp. 248 – 49.

πάλιν

pp. 752 – 53, *pp.* 606 – 7

ADVERB

1. again, once more, anew, also, furthermore, thereupon; **S, P,** or **NLR** [2, 3]

2. on the other hand, in turn; **Alt, Adv, S-R,** or **NLR** [4]

παρά

pp. 756 – 58, *pp. 609 – 11*

PREPOSITION WITH GENITIVE

1. from (the side of); **L** [A1, 3a] *[I.1, 3]*
2. from, by; **L, M-Ed,** or **C-E** [A2] *[I.2][23]*
3. from; **NLR** [A3b] *[I.4]*

PREPOSITION WITH DATIVE

1. at, by, beside, near, with, among, before; **L** [B1, 2, 5] *[II.1, 2a, b, e]*
2. with; **L** or **Ft-In** [B3, 4] *[II.2c, d]*

PREPOSITION WITH ACCUSATIVE

1. by, along, near, at, on; **L** [C1] *[III.1]*
2. during, from ... to (no NT reference); **T** [C2] *[III.2]*
3. in comparison to, rather than, more than, beyond; **//, -/+,** or **NLR** [C3] *[III.3][24]*
4. except for, almost; **C?-E** or **NLR** [C4] *[III.4]*
5. for, because of; **G** [C5] *[III.5]*
6. against, contrary to (rare: Gal 1:8); **Ft-In, Adv,** or **NLR** [C6] *[C.VI]*

Wallace — normal use of the comparative adjective, p. 299; spatial diagram, p. 358; basic uses and significant passages, p. 378; Mark 3:21 and παρά, p. 403; table of NT agency, p. 432; ultimate agent with passive voice, p. 433.

Harris [pp. 171 – 77] — basic sense, p. 171; transferred meanings, pp. 171 – 72; παρὰ (τῷ) θεῷ, pp. 172 – 73; παρά and Christology in the Fourth Gospel, pp. 173 – 76; παρά in compounds, pp. 176 – 77.

---

23. In some situations perhaps [3aγ] *[I.3ac]* may also be categorized under these logical relationships.

24. Παρά may denote a kind of comparison (//), as, e.g., in Heb 2:7: "lower *than* the angels" (i.e., "not *as* high *as* the angels"); or a neg./pos. relationship (-/+), as, e.g., in Rom 1:25: "worshiped and served the creature *rather than* the Creator" (i.e., "worshiped and served the creature *and not* the Creator"). Cf. Harris, pp. 171 – 72.

παραπλήσιον

▲ see παραπλήσιος, ία, ιον p. 770, *p. 621*

NEUTER ADJECTIVE USED AS A PREPOSITION WITH DATIVE[25]

1. coming near, similar (rare: Phil 2:27); **L** or **W-Ed**

Harris — chart of "improper" prepositions in Hellenistic Greek, p. 242; παραπλήσιον, p. 249.

παραπλησίως

▲ p. 770, *p. 621*

ADVERB

1. similarly, likewise, in just the same way (rare: Heb 2:14); //[26]

παρεκτός

▲ p. 774, *p. 625*

ADVERB

1. besides, outside (rare: 2 Cor 11:28); **NLR** [1]

USED AS A PREPOSITION WITH GENITIVE

1. apart from, except for; **C?-E** [2][27]

Harris — chart of "improper" prepositions in Hellenistic Greek, p. 242; παρεκτός, p. 249.

πέραν

▲ pp. 796 – 97, *pp. 643 – 44*

ADVERB

1. the other side (in the construction εἰς τὸ πέραν); **L** [a] *[1]*

---

25. BDAG identifies this as a neuter adjective used as an adverb.

26. The one occurrence of this adverb in the NT is embedded in an inference and therefore difficult to separate usefully, but we list its logical function here nevertheless.

27. Exceptions function as negative conditions: "If not [i.e., except] for this or that instance, X would always be true."

USED AS A PREPOSITION WITH GENITIVE
1. on/to the other side; **L** [b] *[2]*

Wallace — the article as a substantiver with adverbs, p. 232.

Harris — chart of "improper" prepositions in Hellenistic Greek, p. 242; πέραν, p. 249.

περί

pp. 797 – 98, *pp.* 644 – 45

PREPOSITION WITH GENITIVE
1. about, concerning, with regard to, with reference to (sometimes with the article; e.g., Col 4:8); **Gn-Sp** or **Ft-In** [1a, b, c, d, e, f, g,[28] h]
2. on account of, because of, for (rare: Luke 19:37;) **G** [1b]

PREPOSITION WITH ACCUSATIVE
1. around, about, near; **L** [2a]
2. about, near; **T** [2b]
3. with, by (rare: Luke 10:40 – 41); **Gn-Sp** or **C-E** [2c]
4. with respect to, with regard to; **Gn-Sp** [2d]

Wallace — spatial diagram, p. 358; basic uses and significant passages, p. 379.

Harris [pp. 179 – 83] — basic and derived meanings, pp. 179 – 82; περὶ ἁμαρτίας/ἁμαρτιῶν, pp. 182 – 83; περί in compounds, p. 183.

πλήν

▲ p. 826, *p. 669*

ADVERB USED AS A CONJUNCTION
1. (indeed …) but, only, however, nevertheless, rather (often μέν … πλήν); **Adv, -/+,** or **Alt** [1a, b, d]

---

28. When used with ἁμαρτία, περί may have the sense of "to take away," "to atone for," "for," or even "as an offering for" (rare: Rom 8:3). In such instances, a Means-End relationship may be plausible; see BDAG [1g].

2. only, in any case, on the other hand, but; **P** [1b, c, e][29]
3. except that (with ὅτι; rare: Acts 20:23); **C?-E** [1d][30]

USED AS A PREPOSITION WITH GENITIVE

1. but, except, apart from (often after negative statements; rare: Mark 12:32); **C?-E** or -/+ [2]

Wallace — independent, contrastive clauses introduced by a coordinating conjunction, p. 657; logical contrastive (adversative) conjunctions, p. 671; logical inferential conjunctions, p. 673.

Harris — chart of "improper" prepositions in Hellenistic Greek, p. 242; πλήν, p. 249.

πλησίον

▲ p. 830, *pp.* 672–73

NEUTER ADJECTIVE USED AS A PREPOSITION WITH GENITIVE

1. near, close (rare: John 4:5); **L** [1b] *[2]*

Wallace — genitive after certain prepositions, p. 136; the article as a substantiver with adverbs, p. 232.

Harris — chart of "improper" prepositions in Hellenistic Greek, p. 242; πλησίον, p. 249.

πόθεν

▲ p. 838, *p.* 680

INTERROGATIVE ADVERB

1. from where(?), how(?), why(?); **Q-A, Gn-Sp,** or **NLR** [1, 2, 3]

---

29. Since πλήν is a "marker of someth. that is contrastingly added for consideration" (BDAG, 826), it may be seen at times to develop further a thought or discourse.

30. Exceptions function as negative conditions: "If not [i.e., except] for this or that instance, X would always be true." See also 1. Below under USED AS A PREPOSITION WITH GENITIVE.

ποῖος, ποία, ποῖον

▲ pp. 843 – 44, *pp. 684 – 85*

INTERROGATIVE PRONOUN

1. what, what kind, what sort; **Gn-Sp** [1aα, γ, 2aβ, γ, bβ]
2. of what kind?, which?, what?; **Q-A** [1aβ, 2aα, γ, bα]

Wallace — interrogative pronouns, pp. 345 – 46.

ποσάκις

▲ p. 855, *p. 694*

ADVERB

1. how often(?), how many times(?); **Q-A** or **NLR**

πόσος, πόση, πόσον

▲ pp. 855 – 56, *p. 694*

CORRELATIVE PRONOUN

1. how great(?), how much(?), how many(?); **Q-A, Gn-Sp,** or **NLR** [1, 2]

Wallace — interrogative pronouns, pp. 345 – 46.

ποταπός, ποταπή, ποταπόν

▲ p. 856, *pp. 694 – 95*

INTERROGATIVE PRONOUN

1. of what sort, of what kind, how; **Gn-Sp** or **NLR**[31]

πότε

▲ p. 856, *p. 695*

INTERROGATIVE ADVERB

1. when(?), how long? (ἕως πότε); **Q-A, Gn-Sp, T,** or **NLR**

---

31. The interrogative ποταπός only appears in the NT in statements or rhetorical questions. It never appears in a question given a direct answer in the discourse.

πότερος, πότερα, πότερον

▲ p. 856, *p. 695*

INTERROGATIVE PRONOUN[32]

1. whether ... or (πότερον ... ἤ; only at John 7:17);
   Gn-Sp or **Alt**

ποῦ

▲ pp. 857 – 58, *p. 696*

INTERROGATIVE PARTICLE[33]

1. where(?), at/to which place(?); **Q-A, Gn-Sp,** or
   NLR [1, 2]

πρίν

▲ p. 863, *p. 701*

ADVERB USED AS A CONJUNCTION
1. before; **T** [a] *[1]*

ADVERB USED AS A PREPOSITION
1. before; **T** [b] *[2]*

Wallace — adverbial, subsequent infinitive of time, p. 596;
anarthrous infinitives with πρίν (ἤ), p. 609.

πρίν (ἤ) + inf.

▲ see πρίν p. 863, *p. 701*

ADVERB USED AS A CONJUNCTION INTRODUCING AN
INFINITIVE
1. before; **T** [aβ] *[1b]*

Wallace — infinitive, adverbial uses, subsequent time,
p. 596; anarthrous infinitives, p. 609.

---

32. BDAG labels this as "an interrog. word."
33. BAGD ('79) lists this word as an "interrog. adv. of place."

πρό

▲ p. 864, *pp. 701 – 2*

PREPOSITION WITH GENITIVE
1. before, in front of, at; **L** [1]
2. earlier than, before; **T** [2]
3. especially, above all; **P** or **NLR** [3]

See also πρὸ τοῦ + inf.

Wallace — basic uses and significant passages, p. 379; adverbial, subsequent infinitive of time, p. 596; dependent, adverbial clauses of time, p. 665.

Harris [pp. 185 – 88] — NT use and basic meaning, p. 185; notable uses, pp. 186 – 87; πρό in compounds, pp. 187 – 88.

πρὸ τοῦ + inf.

▲ see πρό p. 864, *pp. 701 – 2*

PREPOSITION WITH GENITIVE ARTICULAR INFINTIVE
1. before; **T** [2]

Wallace — infinitive, adverbial uses, subsequent time, p. 596.

πρός

pp. 873 – 75, *pp. 709 – 11*

PREPOSITION WITH GENITIVE
1. to the advantage of (rare: Acts 27:34); **NLR** [1] *[I]*

PREPOSITION WITH DATIVE
1. near, at, by, around; **L** [2a] *[II.1]*

PREPOSITION WITH ACCUSATIVE
1. to, toward, by, at, near, with; **L** [3a, g] *[III.1, 7]*
2. near, at, during, for; **T** [3b] *[III.2]*
3. for, for the purpose of, on behalf of, so that, in order to; **M-Ed** or **C-E** [3c, eε] *[III.3, 5e]*
4. against, for, to, towards, with, before (of relationship); **L** or **Gn-Sp** [3d] *[III.4]*

5. as far as ... is concerned, with respect/reference/regard to, in accordance with; **Gn-Sp, Ft-In,** or **W-Ed** [3eα, β, δ] *[III.5a, b, d]*

See also πρὸς τό + inf.

Wallace — spatial diagram, p. 358; example of motion and state using πρός, pp. 358 – 59; basic uses and significant passages, pp. 380 – 82; adverbial purpose uses of the infinitive, pp. 590 – 91; articular infinitives: πρὸς τό, p. 611.

Harris [pp. 189 – 97] — NT use and basic meaning, pp. 189 – 90; notable instances, pp. 190 – 97; πρός in compounds, p. 197.

πρὸς τό + inf.

▲ see πρός pp. 873 – 75, *pp. 709 – 11*

PREPOSITION WITH ACCUSATIVE ARTICULAR INFINITIVE
1. for, in order to, for the purpose of; **M-Ed** or **C-E** [3cα, εε] *[III.3a, 5e]*

Wallace — infinitive, adverbial uses, purpose, p. 591; articular infinitives, p. 611.

πρῶτος, πρώτη, πρῶτον

pp. 892 – 94, *pp. 725 – 26*

ORDINAL NUMBER SOMETIMES USED AS AN ADVERB
1. first (esp. at the beginning of a sequence or list); **P** or **NLR** [1aβ, b, 2b] *[1b, 2]*

Wallace — adverbial accusative (accusative of manner), p. 201; adverbial use of the adjective, p. 293.

πῶς

▲ pp. 900 – 901, *p. 732*

INTERROGATIVE ADVERB
1. how(?); **Q-A, Gn-Sp,** or **NLR** [1]

σύν

pp. 961 – 62; *pp. 781 – 82*

PREPOSITION WITH DATIVE

1. with, beside; **L, Gn-Sp,** or **W-Ed** [1, 2, 3a, c] *[1, 2, 3, 4, 6]*
2. besides, in addition to; **P** or -/+ (i.e., *"not only this, but also ..."*) [3b] *[5]*

Wallace — the relation of μετά to σύν, pp. 377 – 78; basic uses (with dative only), p. 382; significant passages involving σύν, p. 382.

Harris [pp. 199 – 205] — original meaning and NT incidence, p. 199; two basic uses, pp. 199 – 200; relation to μετά, p. 200; σὺν Χριστῷ and equivalents in Paul, pp. 200 – 204; σύν in compounds, pp. 204 – 5.

τέ

p. 993, *p. 807*

ENCLITIC PARTICLE

1. and, and likewise, and so, so; **S, P, Gn-Sp, W-Ed, C-E,** or **S-R** [1, 2a] *[1]*

Wallace — common Greek coordinating conjunctions, p. 669.

τὲ ... καί

see τέ p. 993, *p. 807*

ENCLITIC PARTICLE COMBINED WITH A CONJUNCTION

1. not only ... but also, and ... and, both ... and; **S, P,** or -/+ [2c] *[3]*

Wallace — no references, but see entries for τέ above and τὲ ... τέ below.

τὲ ... τέ

see τέ p. 993, *p. 807*

Enclitic particle combined with another enclitic
particle

1. both ... and, as ... so, not only ... but also; **S, P,** or -/+
   [2b] *[2]*

Wallace — see τέ entry, above; logical correlative (paired)
conjunctions, p. 672.

τίς, τί

pp. 1006 – 7, *pp. 818 – 19*

Interrogative pronoun

1. who?, which?, what?; **Q-A, Gn-Sp, S-R,** or
   NLR [1a] *[1]*[34]

Neuter pronoun used as an adverb

1. why?; **Q-A, Gn-Sp, S-R, C?-E,** or **NLR** [2] *[3a]*[35]

Wallace — interrogative pronouns, pp. 345 – 46;
see also deliberative subjunctive (*real* and *rhetorical*),
pp. 465 – 68.

---

34. These are the most common and typical logical relationships signaled
by the use of τίς. The interrogative pronoun may also be used in other kinds of
logical relationships, especially when it appears in rhetorical questions. When
an interrogative pronoun is used in a rhetorical question, the rhetorical question should be rephrased as a direct statement, the logical function of which
must be determined by attending to other contextual factors. So, e.g., in Mark
2:7, the question "Who [τίς] can forgive sins, if not [εἰ μή] God alone?" can be
rephrased as a C?-E statement: "No one can forgive sins [E], if not God alone
[C?]."

35. Because of the nature of this word, it can be used to introduce a ground
clause (G). So, e.g., in Gal 3:19, the question "Why the law?" is answered by
"Because of transgressions." Formally, this is a question-answer relationship
(Q-A), but it may also be understood as a logical main clause followed by a
ground clause (G).

τοιγαροῦν

▲ p. 1009, *p. 821*

PARTICLE USED AS A CONJUNCTION
1. therefore, then, for that very reason; ∵

Wallace — logical inferential conjunctions, p. 673.

τοίνυν

▲ p. 1009, *p. 821*

PARTICLE USED AS A CONJUNCTION
1. hence, so, indeed, therefore, then; ∵

Wallace — logical inferential conjunctions, p. 673.

τοιοῦτος, τοιαύτη, τοιοῦτον

pp. 1009 – 10, *p. 821*

CORRELATIVE ADJECTIVE
1. such, of such a kind, like such (rare: Acts 26:29); //,
    Ft-In, or **Gn-Sp** [a] *[1]*

See also entry for οἷος, οἵα, οἷον *above.*

ADJECTIVE
1. such (followed by a relative clause); **Ft-In** [bɔ] *[2aγ]*

τοσοῦτος, τοσαύτη, τοσοῦτον

p. 1012, *p. 823*

CORRELATIVE ADJECTIVE
1. so much, as much (rare: Heb 1:4); // [2a, 5] *[1aα, 2bγ]*

See also entry for ὅσος, ὅση, ὅσον *above.*

τότε

pp. 1012 – 13, *pp. 823 – 24*

CORRELATIVE ADVERB
1. then (as a main clause referring back to a temporal
    clause; e.g., 2 Cor 12:10); **T** [1c]
2. then, thereupon; **P, C-E,** ∵, or **S-R** [2]

τοὐναντίον[36]

▲ see ἐναντίον p. 330, *pp. 261 – 62*

PARTICLE USED AS AN ADVERB

1. on the other hand (rare: Gal 2:7); **NLR** [2][37]

ὑπέρ

pp. 1030 – 31, *pp. 838 – 39*

PREPOSITION WITH GENITIVE

1. for, in behalf of, in place of, in the name of, instead of, for the sake of; **Gn-Sp, L,**[38] or **NLR** [A1a, c] *[1a, c]*
2. in order to; **M-Ed** [A1b] *[1b]*
3. because of, for, for the sake of; **G** [A2] *[1d]*
4. about, concerning, with reference to; **Ft-In** or **Gn-Sp** [A3] *[1f]*

PREPOSITION WITH ACCUSATIVE

1. over and above, more than, than, beyond; **Gn-Sp, L, //,** or **NLR** [B] *[2]*

PREPOSITION USED AS AN ADVERB

1. even more (rare: 2 Cor 11:23); **NLR** [C] *[3]*

Wallace — normal usage of the comparative adjective, p. 299; spatial diagram, p. 358; significant passages involving ἀντί in comparison with ὑπέρ, pp. 365 – 68; basic uses and significant passages, pp. 383 – 89.

---

36. τοὐναντίον = the definite article ὁ + the neuter adjective ἐναντίον.

37. Semantically, this word expresses some kind of contrast. However, in actual NT usage the word is always accompanied by another and more specific marker of a contrastive relationship, which it enforces.

38. In some NT instances, the preposition may be relationally locative. See BDAG, 1030: "The loc. sense 'over, above' is not found in our lit ... but does appear in nonliteral senses." Note also Harris' introductory comment: "The commonest meaning of this preposition ('on behalf of') seems to have arisen from the image of one person standing or bending *over* another in order to shield or protect them, or of a shield lifted *over* the head that suffers the blow instead of the person" (207, emphasis original).

Harris [pp. 207 – 17] — original meaning and NT use, p. 207; ὑπέρ with the accusative, pp. 207 – 9; ὑπέρ with the genitive, pp. 209 – 10; ὑπέρ and περί, pp. 210 – 11; ὑπέρ meaning "in the place of," pp. 211 – 15; ὑπέρ as expressing both representation/advantage and substitution, pp. 215 – 16; ὑπέρ in compounds, p. 217.

ὑπεράνω

▲ p. 1032, *p. 840*

ADVERB USED AS A PREPOSITION WITH GENITIVE
1. (high) above; L

Wallace — genitive after certain prepositions, p. 136.

Harris — chart of "improper" prepositions in Hellenistic Greek, pp. 240, 242; ὑπεράνω, pp. 249 – 50.

ὑπερέκεινα

▲ p. 1032, *p. 840*

ADVERB USED AS A PREPOSITION WITH GENITIVE
1. beyond; L or NLR

Harris — chart of "improper" prepositions in Hellenistic Greek, p. 242; ὑπερέκεινα, p. 250.

ὑπό

pp. 1035 – 36, *p. 843*

PREPOSITION WITH GENITIVE
1. by; M-Ed or C-E [A] *[1]*

PREPOSITION WITH ACCUSATIVE
1. under, below (spatially or relationally); L [B1, 2] *[2a, b]*
2. about (rare: Acts 5:21); T [B3] *[2c]*

Wallace — the genitive of agency, p. 126; how agency is expressed in the NT, pp. 164 – 66; spatial diagram, p. 358; basic uses and significant passages, p. 389; table of NT agency expression, p. 432; ultimate agency, pp. 433 – 34.

Harris [pp. 219 – 23] — original meaning and NT use, p. 219; ὑπό with the accusative, pp. 219 – 20; ὑπό with the genitive, p. 220; ὑπὸ νόμον, pp. 220 – 21; ὑπό and other prepositions expressing agency, pp. 221 – 23; ὑπό in compounds, p. 223.

ὑποκάτω

▲ p. 1038, *p. 844*

ADVERB USED AS A PREPOSITION WITH GENITIVE
1. under, below, down at; L

Wallace — genitive after certain prepositions, p. 136.

Harris — chart of "improper" prepositions in Hellenistic Greek, pp. 240, 242; ὑποκάτω, p. 250.

ὕστερον

▲ see ὕστερος, ὕστερα, ὕστερον p. 1044, *p. 849*

NEUTER ADJECTIVE USED AS AN ADVERB
1. finally; P or NLR [2bβ]

Wallace — adverbial use of the adjective, p. 293.

χάριν

▲ pp. 1078 – 79, *p. 877*

ACCUSATIVE NOUN USED AS A PREPOSITION WITH GENITIVE
1. for the sake of, for this purpose (sometimes with τούτου); M-Ed [a] *[1]*
2. for this reason, therefore (sometimes with οὗ; cf. entries ὅς, ἥ, ὅ and οὗ χάριν above); ∴ or G[39] [b] *[2]*

Harris — chart of "improper" prepositions in Hellenistic Greek, p. 242; χάριν, p. 250.

---

39. Χάριν phrases at times point forward to a following clause, providing a basis or ground (G). See, e.g., 1 John 3:12; in this instance, the clause in which χάριν appears is not itself the ground clause but introduces it.

χωρίς

p. 1095, *pp. 890–91*

ADVERB
1. separately, apart, by itself; **NLR** [1]

USED AS A PREPOSITION WITH GENITIVE
1. without, apart from, independent(ly of); **L** or
   Gn-Sp [2aα, bα, δ]
2. without, apart from, besides, except for; **C?-E**[40] or
   L [2aβ, γ, bβ, γ]
3. apart from (rare: 2 Cor 11:28); -/+ [2bε]

Harris — chart of "improper" prepositions in Hellenistic
Greek, p. 242; χωρίς, pp. 250–51; notable uses of selected
"improper" prepositions: χωρίς, pp. 263–65.

ὧδε

p. 1101, *p. 895*

ADVERB
1. here, in this case, under these circumstances;
   Ft-In [2] [2b]

ὡς

pp. 1103–6, *pp. 897–99*

RELATIVE ADVERB USED AS A COMPARATIVE PARTICLE OR
CONJUNCTION
1. as, like (sometimes combined with οὕτως); // or
   W-Ed [1, 2, 3aα, γ, b, c] [I, II, III.1a, c, 2, 3]
2. as, because; **G** [3aβ] [III.1b]
3. so that (rare: Heb 3:11); **C-E** [4] [IV.2]
4. how, that, the fact that; **Gn-Sp** [5] [IV.4]
5. about, approximately, nearly; **Ft-In, T,** or
   NLR [6] [IV.5]
6. how!; **NLR** [7] [IV.6]

---

40. Exceptions function as negative conditions: "If not [i.e., except] for this
or that instance, X would always be true."

7. when, after, while, as long, since, as soon as (sometimes with ἄν; see entry above; also ὡς ἄν below); T [8] [IV.1]
8. with a view to, in order to; M-Ed [9a, b] [IV.3a, b]
9. as (pertaining to direction; rare: Acts 17:14 [variant]); L [9c] [IV.3c]

Wallace — ὡς and the substantival double-accusative, p. 184; adverbial use of the infinitive expressing purpose, pp. 590 – 91, and result, pp. 592 – 93; ὡς + the anarthrous infinitive, p. 609; common Greek subordinating conjunctions, p. 669; adverbial conjunctions: causal, p. 674, comparative, p. 675, result, p. 677, temporal, p. 677; substantival content conjunctions, p. 678.

ὡς + inf.

see ὡς p. 1106, *p. 898*

RELATIVE ADVERB USED AS A CONJUNCTION INTRODUCING AN INFINITIVE

1. in order to, for the purpose of, so that; M-Ed [9b] [IV.3b]

Wallace — infinitive, adverbial uses, purpose, pp. 590 – 91; anarthrous infinitives, p. 609.

ὡς ἄν

see ὡς p. 1106, *p. 898*; also ὡς ἄν or ὡσάν p. 1106, *p. 899*

RELATIVE ADVERB AND PARTICLE USED AS A CONJUNCTION
1. when, whenever, as soon as; T (ὡς [8c] [IV.1c])
2. as if, as it were, so to speak; W-Ed [ὡς ἄν or ὡσάν]

Wallace — adverbial temporal conjunctions, p. 677.

ὡσαύτως

▲ p. 1106, *p. 899*

ADVERB

1. (in) the same (way), similarly, likewise; **S, P, //, W-Ed,** or **NLR**

Wallace — adverbial comparative (manner) conjunctions, p. 675.

ὡσεί

▲ p. 1106, *p. 899*

CONJUNCTION

1. as, like; // [1]
2. about; **NLR** [2]

Wallace — adverbial comparative (manner) conjunctions, p. 675.

ὥσπερ

pp. 1106 – 7, *p. 899*

CONJUNCTION

1. (just) as ..., so (sometimes followed by οὕτως καί, or combined with οὖν); // [a, b] [1, 2]

Wallace — adverbial comparative (manner) conjunctions, p. 675.

ὡσπερεί

▲ p. 1107, *p. 899*

CONJUNCTION

1. like, as though, as it were; //

ὥστε

p. 1107, *pp. 899 – 900*

CONJUNCTION

1. for this reason, therefore, so; ∴ [1]
2. so that, for the purpose of, with a view to, in order that; **M-Ed** or **C-E** [2]

Wallace — adverbial use of the infinitive of purpose, pp. 590 – 91, result, pp. 592 – 93; independent clauses introduced by an inferential coordinating conjunction, p. 658; logical inferential conjunctions, p. 673; adverbial result conjunctions, p. 677.

ὥστε + inf.

see ὥστε p. 1107, *p. 900*

CONJUNCTION INTRODUCING AN INFINITIVE

1. so that; **C-E** [2aβ]
2. in order to, for the purpose of, so that; **M-Ed** or **C-E** [2b]

Wallace — infinitive, adverbial uses, purpose, pp. 590 – 91; result, 592 – 93; anarthrous infinitives, p. 610.